Happiness 101

Happiness 101:

18 Lessons for Latter-day Saints on How to Live a Happier Life!

By
Gregory R. Wille

Horizon
Springville, Utah

ISBN 13: 978-0-88290-950-9

Published by Horizon, an imprint of Cedar Fort, Inc., 2373 W. 700 S., Springville, UT 84663
Distributed by Cedar Fort, Inc., www.cedarfort.com

LIBRARY OF CONGRESS CATALOGING-IN-PUBLICATION DATA
Wille, Gregory R., 1947-
 Happiness 101 / Gregory R. Wille.
 p. cm.
 ISBN 978-0-88290-950-9
 1. Happiness--Religious aspects--Church of Jesus Christ of Latter-day
Saints. 2. Christian life--Mormon authors. I. Title.
 BX8643.H35W55 2008
 248.4'89332--dc22
 2008025092
Cover design by Angela Olsen
Cover design © 2008 by Lyle Mortimer
Edited and typeset by Jessica Best and Laura Mathews

Printed in the United States of America

10 9 8 7 6 5 4 3 2 1

Printed on acid-free paper

Table of Contents

Part 4: A Happier Life Through Greater Social Well-Being

Part 5: A Happier Life Through Greater Spiritual Well-Being

Part 6: A Happier Life Through Greater Emotional Well-Being

Also by Gregory R. Wille
Now, What Do You Believe?

Preface

I received my patriarchal blessing just before entering the mission field at the age of nineteen. In this marvelous blessing the patriarch counseled me to prayerfully seek my personal mission in life. There is a special work that the Lord wants me to accomplish here in mortality, just as there is a special work that He wants you to accomplish here on earth.

Over my lifetime, I have prayerfully contemplated and sought to discover what personal gifts and talents I have received from the Lord, and what my personal mission might be by which I might use these gifts and talents to further His purposes. Over time, it gradually came to me that *my* personal mission is much the same as *your* personal mission, and the personal mission or calling of every other faithful Latter-day Saint. It is actually a two-part mission that you and I have been given by the Lord to accomplish in this life. It is as follows:

My Personal Mission Statement

My overarching goal or mission in life is to live worthy to return back to my Heavenly Father and to my Savior at life's end, and to take my wife, my family, and as many other individuals as I possibly can with me in the process.

My second primary or overarching goal or mission in life is to experience as much joy and happiness in traveling the road back to God as I possibly can, and along the way, to bring as much happiness into the lives of others as I possibly can. I will serve, I will lift, I will love.

Now why, do you suppose, my greatest desire in life is to return back to the presence of my Heavenly Father? Is it yours? Are the two overarching goals listed above somehow related?

In the scriptures the "plan of salvation" and the "plan of happiness" are terms that are often used interchangeably and mean the same thing. So why do we seek salvation? Because we are seeking happiness! Indeed, we are seeking to obtain the greatest feelings of happiness that exist in the universe—even a "fullness of joy." We are told that "this is a joy which none receiveth save it be the truly penitent and humble seeker of happiness" (Alma 27:18). Are you a "truly penitent and humble seeker of happiness," or in other words, salvation?

If you greatly dislike washing dirty dishes and knew that in the next life your eternal assignment would be washing other people's dirty dishes in some heavenly kitchen and that you would be eternally miserable doing it, how great would your desire be to return to God's presence? Probably not too great. But is that what God promises you and me? No, He promises His faithful children an eternity of happiness, joy, and bliss. We base our faith, our obedience, and our hope on His promise that we can one day obtain this ultimate state of happiness and joy.

This book was written to help you and me achieve our primary goals or overarching mission in life as previously described. That is, to gain as much happiness in this life as we possibly can, while proving ourselves worthy to gain the ultimate feelings of happiness and joy in the life to come. Our entire purpose for existence is based on achieving and experiencing feelings of true happiness. Yes, "men are [they exist], that they might have joy" (2 Nephi 2:25).

In this life we know that our feelings of happiness can be quite fleeting. Unhappiness can come into our lives from many directions. It may come from boredom, fatigue, loneliness, envy, guilt, fear, or any one of a host of other negative conditions or experiences. Unpleasant events, unbalanced hormones, rainy days, and bad hair days can put us in a bad mood, and at times, we each have trials and sorrows to deal with. But even so, with a clear understanding of the gospel of Jesus Christ, it is possible for everyone to increase feelings of happiness in their life. My hope is that this book will help you do just that.

x

Introduction

"I Just Want to Feel Happy" . . . A Universal Desire

I know something about you. Yes, even though I may never have met you, I know something deeply personal and extremely important about you. What is it, you ask? Well, listen closely. I know that happiness is something that you greatly desire. In fact, seeking to capture feelings of happiness is the main motivation for nearly everything you think, say, or do.

You may wonder how I knew. Am I psychic? Do I have a crystal ball? Did I discover this great secret of yours from talking to your mother? No. I know this great truth about you because I know that acquiring feelings of happiness is something that everyone desires. We all want to capture those elusive little bluebirds of happiness.

> How to gain, how to keep, how to recover happiness is in fact for most men at all times the secret motive of all they do, and of all they are willing to endure.
>
> ~William James

In this book I will be talking a lot about little bluebirds of happiness, because I have learned that true happiness must be achieved a little bit at a time. You don't set out to capture just one gigantic bird, but lots of little birds. That might not make much sense to you right now, but keep reading and soon you'll understand what I mean.

People have been trying to capture those remarkable little bluebirds since the beginning of time. In fact, according to the ancient Greek philosopher Aristotle, the one thing that men and women seek more than any other thing is happiness. He taught that "while happiness itself is sought for its own sake, every other goal—health, beauty, money, or power—is valued only because we expect that it will make us happy."[1]

This principle holds true today just as much as it did in Aristotle's day. At different times in your life you may seek after a trip to Hawaii, a promotion at work, a new "toy" to play with, or a date for Friday night. In each case, the underlying reason why you seek these things is in hopes of increasing your personal happiness. In fact, virtually everything you do is in hopes of increasing your well-being or happiness. Makes sense, doesn't it?

> Happiness is the supreme object of existence.
> ~J. Gilchrist Lawson

In a moment, I will be introducing you to eighteen principles which, if properly applied, are virtually guaranteed to increase feelings of happiness in your life. First things first, however. As we begin our discussion, it will be beneficial if we first answer the question: What is happiness?

What Is Happiness?

To experience feelings of happiness in your life, you do not need to be walking around with a huge smile on your face every moment or be jumping up and down for joy every minute of the day. Of course, it's wonderful to have those moments in our lives when we feel extremely, fantastically happy and joyful. But personal experience teaches us that such moments in life are more often the exception rather than the rule. The feelings of happiness we enjoy in life are usually much more subdued and subtle than this—but even so, they are wonderful.

Psychologists often describe happiness as a feeling of contentment or fulfillment, or a sense of well-being. As members of the Church we often take this a step higher and also associate happiness with feelings of inner peace, love, celestial joy, and humble gratitude. Happiness includes a whole range of positive emotions. "Happiness is an emotion associated with feelings ranging from contentment and satisfaction to bliss and intense joy."[2]

Some speak of happiness as a true freedom of mind and spirit that comes from a feeling of control over one's own life and destiny. It was this understanding that caused America's founding fathers to tie the principles of individual freedom and liberty to yet another of man's inalienable, God-given rights: "the pursuit of happiness." In other words, if you are free to make your own choices in life, you are going to be a lot happier than if you are forced against your will to do things that you really don't want to do.

This explains why we punish a man by putting him in jail, and we punish a child by sending him to his room or by taking away certain privileges temporarily. In each case we restrict the individual's personal freedom, thus denying him the opportunity to pursue or participate in those activities in which he would normally find some degree of happiness. With a loss of freedom comes a corresponding loss of happiness. This is why we yearn for freedom, and why God gave us moral agency. It is because the principle of freedom is so closely associated with the attainment of happiness.

Some writers define happiness as a state of mind free from unhappiness. Although such a definition may seem obvious or simplistic, it is an important concept to understand, for it shows us that we can approach our pursuit of happiness in two different ways. First, we can learn from others what makes them happy and then actively incorporate these same positive behaviors in our own lives to see if they work for us. Second, we can search for and then, one-by-one, begin to eliminate from our lives those things that we discover are making us unhappy. Using either, or preferably both techniques, we can become happier.

No matter how someone wishes to describe it, we know that happiness, originates from within us. Although it is a feeling or state of mind that is somewhat difficult to define, we all know it when we feel it.

How to Capture Those Elusive Little Bluebirds of Happiness

Imagine yourself waking up one morning to a strange sound coming from the backyard. As you sleepily peer out the bedroom

3

window you discover a cheerful singing bluebird resting on the patio, greeting the new day. Never before in your life have you ever seen an actual bluebird or heard its happy song, and you are anxious for your whole family to experience this remarkable sight and sound. In your half-awake state, not thinking too clearly, you conclude that you must capture this beautiful wonder of nature!

You slowly open the back door of the house and inch toward the creature. As you draw close to the bird it hops away, maintaining about a ten foot barrier between the two of you. As you continue to creep toward the bird it begins to lead you in circles around the yard. After several minutes of this silly game you become frustrated and decide you have had enough of this. You emit a wild screech and frantically charge the bird. With arms outstretched you run at full speed directly toward the fowl, only to watch in dismay as it quickly lifts off the ground, wings its way out of reach, and in a few moments disappears totally from your sight.

This episode is exactly what happens to so many people who attempt to capture happiness. No matter how fast or how determined they are, they cannot capture the bluebird of happiness by running directly toward it. By doing so, the bird (happiness) evades and eludes them every time.

You will never capture a bluebird of happiness by simply running toward it. You have to outsmart it. You have coax that elusive little bird to you. Instead of looking directly at the bird (that is, happiness, your primary goal or objective), you must focus your attention on secondary goals. For example, you may want to begin your pursuit of happiness by improving your health and getting your physical body in better shape. A month into your fitness program you will sit down one day to rest and notice how much better you are feeling. In this relaxed condition it will suddenly dawn on you that there is a little bluebird sitting on your shoulder, singing merrily away. This realization may surprise you at first. You were so focused on your exercise program and your new, healthier diet that you weren't even aware of the bird's presence, even though it has been perched on your shoulder for over a week.

Now that you have begun to improve your health and are starting to feel better physically, you decide it's time to begin on another secondary goal: improving your finances by getting out of debt. Several months into your new, improved financial program, you find that you are no longer losing sleep worrying about how the bills will be paid at the first of each month. Then one day, you sit down on the couch to relax and begin to meditate about your current situation in life and how things are going. Suddenly you hear the vaguely familiar chirping of a little bird. You look to your side and, lo and behold, there you see a second little bluebird sitting on your shoulder. Once again, you have achieved your primary goal! You wonder how long the bird has been there. You have been so focused on achieving your secondary goals of better health and improved finances that you hadn't even noticed the two little bluebirds perched on your shoulder.

Two little bluebirds sitting on your shoulder feels great—you definitely feel happier. If you feel so much better by having coaxed two birds to you, just imagine how fantastic you would feel if you had a dozen or more of these cute little birds singing on your shoulders.

Eighteen Happiness Principles

Recent scientific studies indicate that a person's "cheer level" is about one-half genetic. In other words, some people just seem to be happier by nature than others. There are certain personality and character traits that each of us bring with us when we enter mortality. We all know people who are bubbly, cheerful, and positive almost all the time, no matter how hard life gets. Now if you are on the other end of the scale—a person who is somewhat grumpy and negative by nature—that can make feeling lots of happiness on a regular basis a little more difficult to achieve. But the good news is that only 50 percent of your "cheer level" is genetic. The other half can be altered or affected by your environment and actions. In other words, even if you are grouchy by nature, you can still increase your feelings of happiness by changing your environment or by actively coaxing little bluebirds of happiness to you.

In the following pages there are eighteen lessons, each teaching a specific happiness principle. If fully implemented, each principle is capable of coaxing a little bluebird onto your shoulder. That is, each principle is capable of increasing the happiness in your life. The more principles you actively make a part of your life, the greater your overall feelings of happiness will be.

These eighteen principles represent secondary goals. Each principle, if fully embraced and put into practice, will help you achieve

> "Men are, that they might have joy."
> ~2 Nephi 2:25

your primary goal of true happiness. As you read through these happiness principles, take a moment at the end of each chapter to think about how the principle just discussed might affect you. Are you already applying this principle in your life? Could your feelings of happiness increase by applying this principle more fully? If you discover a principle that you feel you need to work on, take some time to develop a specific plan or strategy for how you might implement this principle more fully in your life, based on your specific needs and desires.

One last but important thought. The comedian Jonathan Winters once stated: "If your ship doesn't come in, swim out to it!"[3] In other words, don't just sit around, hoping that someday the bluebirds of happiness will land on your shoulders. If you do, those elusive little birds may pass you by altogether. If a feeling of greater happiness is what you really want to experience in life, you need to go after it. You need to study, and then begin to actively put into practice, those principles that will lead you to greater happiness. Reading this book will be of little value to you if you don't apply these happiness principles in your life.

Good luck on your pursuit of happiness! Let's begin. Here is your first lesson on how to capture a little bluebird.

Notes
1. As quoted in Mihaly Csikszentmihalyi's *Flow*, p. 1.
2. http://en.wikipedia.org/wiki/Enjoyment.
3. www.quotationspage.com/quote/29688.html.

Part One:

Getting Started

Happiness Principle #1:

Determine what activities make you personally the happiest, and then make them the center of your life

Every person is unique. The things I like to eat, read, and do, are probably different from what you like to eat, read, and do. Your talents and abilities are different from mine. You are better at doing some things than I am, and I am better at doing some things than you are.

People who describe themselves as being very happy or extremely happy have usually taken the time to figure out exactly what it is they enjoy doing the most. They then work to make those activities the center of their lives. They organize their time, giving highest priority to those activities that bring them the greatest fulfillment, peace, and happiness.

Very happy people tend to enjoy a large variety of activities. Their interests are greatly diversified. On the other hand, less happy people usually have only a few interests. For example, perhaps a man's only passion is snow skiing. That's great because this will provide him with some wonderful winter fun. But, unfortunately, this will also lead him to some terribly long, boring summers. The more interests you develop, the less time you will spend feeling bored, and the more time you will spend experiencing feelings of happiness.

One word of caution. Increasing your happiness in life is not just about increasing the amount of fun you experience. Having a fun time is great, but it usually lasts just a few minutes or hours. Achieving true happiness is much more permanent in nature and goes deeper than just having a good laugh once in awhile. You should be aware that a total diet of either recreation or work can distract or divert you from pursuing the more important aspects of life, such as developing close personal relationships with family members, with friends, and with God. To maximize your feelings of happiness you need to live a balanced life. Don't allow your pursuit of recreation, fun, or the almighty dollar cause you to become unbalanced. Maximize your happiness by developing all aspects of your character and life—the physical, mental, emotional, spiritual, social, and financial.

> If I had my life to live over, I would start barefoot earlier in the spring and stay that way later in the fall. I would go to more dances. I would ride more merry-go-rounds. I would pick more daisies.
>
> ~Nadine Stair

With these thoughts in mind, take some time to think about and write down those activities that you enjoy doing the most. Then center your life around them. To start you thinking, here are a few activities (not material things) that I have on my happy list:

1. Being with my wife: helping her find happiness and fulfillment

2. Enjoying my children: supporting their growth and happiness

3. Attending the temple, worship services, and other Church activities

4. Seeing new places, experiencing new activities

5. Working out each morning: jogging, exercising

6. Listening to uplifting, classical, and sacred music

7. Reading self-improvement books

8. Taking classes, reading books, learning new skills in areas of interest

9. Playing basketball in the driveway with my boys

10. Skiing, river rafting, camping, working in the yard

11. Studying the scriptures, meditating, praying

12. Being involved in a good cause (such as missionary work)

13. Having friends to dinner or other fun activities

14. Enjoying lakes, rivers, mountains, and oceans

15. Attending cultural and sporting events

16. Experiencing creative, fulfilling work

I enjoy each of these activities, not necessarily because of the nature of the activity itself, but because of the *positive feelings* each provides me with. I feel an increase of love when serving God, my family, and my fellow man. I feel awe as I study the beauty of a flower, a sunset, or a mountain forest. I feel excitement when skiing down a mountain or rafting a river. I feel curiosity and fascination when visiting a new place or reading a good book. I feel peace when studying the scriptures and praying. All of these positive emotions add to, and are associated with, an underlying feeling of happiness. Each activity enriches and adds quality to my life experience.

The more time we spend doing the things we truly enjoy, the happier we will feel. When we don't have or don't make the time to participate in these positive activities, our feelings of happiness will suffer.

Take the case of Bill, for example. Bill spent eight to ten hours a day working at a job he greatly disliked. He spent nearly two hours a day commuting to and from work in rush hour traffic—something he hated to do. Evenings and weekends were often spent in doing yard work, running errands, or other jobs that he really didn't like to do either. At other times, with few interests to occupy his time, he often felt tired or bored. In fact, his mental health counselor determined that Bill spent approximately 80 to 90 percent of his waking hours doing things that he either hated or just didn't like. The other 10 to 20 percent of his time was spent on activities that he felt neutral about (such as eating and bathing). Little wonder that Bill had come in to receive treatment for depression.

What about you? What percentage of your waking hours is spent on doing things you really enjoy? What percentage of time do you spend on activities you greatly dislike? How much time do you spend on activities you feel somewhat neutral about? Hopefully you aren't a Bill, but could you arrange your schedule so that you spend more time on activities that you love doing?

Just recently, to broaden and diversify my own knowledge and interests in life, I spent one evening a week for six weeks taking a landscaping design class at the local county agricultural extension service. I learned some great things about plants and gardens and landscaping. Since I don't presently have enough money to do all the landscaping improvements on my yard that I would like to do, I have drawn up a five-year plan. Each spring and autumn I have plans for improvements I want to make to one section of the yard. It's fun and satisfying to use my creative abilities in designing a beautiful flower bed or garden area. This activity adds to my feelings of happiness.

If you want to increase your feelings of happiness, be sure to take the time to make your own list of happy activities. Decide on some new ones to try. Then organize your life so you have more time to enjoy them.

Happiness Principle #2:

Simplify your life

When life gets too complicated, when too many demands are placed upon us, it can definitely reduce our feelings of peace and happiness.

Of course, a certain amount of stress in our lives is actually necessary for our growth and happiness. The natural stresses created by working for a livelihood or as a homemaker, performing the normal duties of a spouse and parent, and magnifying a Church calling are positive in nature and benefit us. If we can handle them, we can, and should, add other activities to our lives that promote growth and happiness. But sometimes we overload ourselves.

On one occasion while serving as a bishop, I had a sister from the ward come into my office for a visit. She wanted to be released from her calling as the eleven-year-old Scout leader. She was doing a wonderful job and seemed to enjoy the boys, and they seemed to enjoy her. I asked her why she wanted to be released. She said she was too stressed and had to relieve some of the pressure from her life. She explained that besides working with the

> Reduce the complexity of life by eliminating the needless wants of life, and the labors of life reduce themselves.
> ~Edwin Way Teale

Scouts, she was the adult leader over a Girl Scout troop; coach of a girl's city league softball team; was involved in several other charities and community service organizations; and worked part-time twenty hours a week, as well as trying to be a homemaker, wife, and a good mother to her four very active children. To keep her sanity, she was giving up her involvement with everything but her family.

Of course I was sad to release her because besides doing a wonderful job, I knew that she had made covenants in the temple to consecrate her time and talents to the Lord for the building up of His Church and kingdom on the earth. The thought came into my mind that it might be better for her to keep her Church calling and unload all her other extra-curricular activities. I didn't vocalize these thoughts, however, because the more we talked, the more I could see that she was on the verge of having a nervous breakdown. I expressed my love and concern for her, and we released her the next Sunday.

Organize your life so that you have the time, the strength, and the energy to take care of those things that are most important, such as family, church, and employment, and then add other activities if you can. If you start to feel overly stressed out, however, take a close look at your life. Determine where the line is that moves you from happiness to unhappiness and then begin eliminating from your life those activities that have pushed you over the line. Learn to say no. You don't have to do everything for everyone. Get back on the happy side of the line and start enjoying life again!

Elaine St. James has written several books on the subject of simplifying your life, including *Simplify Your Life* and *Living the Simple Life*. In her writings, she talks about reducing, if necessary, the number of stressful commitments in our lives, and she describes her own experiences in eliminating or reducing time spent on the more mundane or less-rewarding activities of life. For example, rather than wash the bed sheets every week, she now washes them every other week. Family members wear their clothes an extra time or two, if they are still basically clean, before throwing them in the laundry. As a result, she only does laundry once instead of twice a week. The time she saves by doing this she spends on more fulfilling activities that she truly enjoys, like painting and writing.

Other time-savers include such things as organizing school car pools, installing a telephone answering machine, and moving closer to work to cut down on commuting time. With a little planning, these, and dozens of similar strategies, can provide you with many extra hours to do the things that you really enjoy doing the most, like all of those happiness-producing activities that you listed for Happiness Principle #1. As a result, your life will become less stressful, more simple, and much richer!

There are still other ways to simplify your life. For example, John owned a horse. When his children were young, they used to have fun riding the horse nearly every day. As the children became teenagers they lost interest in the horse. Still John would go out and water and feed the horse all winter long. One day when it was about twenty degrees below zero, as he was breaking through the ice in the horse's water trough, a light bulb turned on in John's brain. He asked himself, "Why am I out here freezing, spending my hard-earned money on hay and oats, and wasting fifteen minutes of my precious time every day, to feed a horse that none of my family members care about or enjoy anymore?" The next day John put an ad in the newspaper and sold the horse. He simplified his life.

> To find the universal elements enough; to find the air and the water exhilarating; to be refreshed by a morning walk or an evening saunter . . . to be thrilled by the stars at night; to be elated over a bird's nest or a wild-flower in spring—these are some of the rewards of the simple life.
>
> ~John Burroughs

Jim lived farther down the road. Jim had really taken to heart the idea of simplifying his life. At one point he had been the owner of the local fast-food restaurant in town. The business afforded his family a good living, but he had to work nearly seventy hours a week to keep the business running smoothly and profitably. One day he woke up and realized that life was passing him by. "Is this all there is to life?" he asked himself. He was successful in business, but was he happy in life? He determined he wasn't.

Jim approached his wife, Susan, with his feelings and she agreed that a major lifestyle change would benefit them both. They sold the business and their large house, with its equally large mortgage, and bought a much smaller house in the country. They questioned why they needed three TV sets and much of the stuff they had accumulated over the years. Between garage sales and donations to friends and thrift stores like Deseret Industries, they rid themselves of many, if not most, of their possessions. They were surprised at the increased feelings of freedom and peace of mind they experienced by not having a mountain of things to maintain or worry about. With the money from these sales they paid off all their debts, which increased their feelings of freedom even more.

Slowing down from their previously fast-paced lifestyle seemed a little strange at first. They actually had time to take walks out in nature as a family! And in the evenings they would sit out in the backyard and enjoy the mountain sunset together—something that Jim had not taken the time to do for years. They also found that they now had more time to spend on church callings, and they began donating some of their new-found extra time to community service down at the local food bank.

> Frugality is one of the most beautiful and joyful words in the English language, and yet one that we are culturally cut off from understanding and enjoying. The consumption society has made us feel that happiness lies in having things, and has failed to teach us the happiness of not having things.
> ~Elise Boulding

Between some investment income, a part-time home business, and his lack of debt, Jim was able to make ends meet. They had to budget carefully, of course, and look for ways to keep expenses down. They could only rarely go out to eat, and they had to rent videos at reduced rates rather than attend movies at the theater. But they knew that their new lifestyle was well worth the sacrifice. They didn't feel deprived; they felt free. Jim now had time to do things he had always wanted to spend more time doing: writing, studying the scriptures deeply, and serving others. It felt good. Jim and Susan had not only simplified their lives, but they had also greatly increased their feelings of happiness.

So you see, there are many different ways to simplify your life. It can involve cutting back on stressful commitments, organizing yourself so as to better utilize your time, or saving both time and money by ridding yourself of unnecessary things. You may not be psychologically ready or in a financial position to take the total plunge into the simple lifestyle that Jim and Susan took. But certainly, with a little thought, you can find a number of ways to simplify, better organize, and enrich your life.

To apply this happiness principle in my own life, I began by cleaning out and organizing my clothes closet. I followed up by organizing my tools and storage items in the garage and basement. Now I no longer waste a bunch of time trying to find our stored Christmas decorations each December. And I know right where to find my handsaw and my Sunday shoes. Every minute I save by being better organized I can now spend on one of the happiness-producing activities on my list. My wife, Shelley, and I also recently put an ad in the newspaper and sold several old toys we rarely use anymore. Now I no longer have to spend time and money to maintain them. I have simplified my life and I am happier for having done so. You can do it too!

Yes, to increase your feelings of happiness, simplify your life. It's as simple as that.

Part Two:

A Happier Life Through Greater Financial Well-Being

Happiness Principle #3:

Understand the relationship between money and happiness

During the priesthood session of the October 2000 general conference of the Church, President Gordon B. Hinckley explained the importance of education and how it relates to a man's ability to earn a good living for his family. Taken from an article by Nicole A. Bonham entitled "Does an Advanced Degree Pay Off?," President Hinckley read the following:

> The latest Census information ... indicated the annual wage for someone without a degree and no high school diploma stood at a little more than $16,000 nationally [in 1997]. The jump wasn't much higher for a high school diploma—$22,895 annual average income. As the level of education increases, however, so does the span. The holder of a bachelor's degree earned, on average, $40,478 that year. Finally, the holder of an advanced degree typically bumped up their annual earnings by more than $20,000 to a nationwide average of $63,229, according to [these] Census figures.[1]

In today's world, getting a good education is critical if someone hopes to earn sufficient income to provide well for his family. And, as we will see in a moment, a sufficient amount of income is essential in helping our family members and ourselves feel secure and happy. In simple terms: a better education leads to a higher income, which in turn can lead to greater happiness.

Money, in and of itself, is neither good nor evil. Certainly we can use it for either purpose, if we wish. In the scriptures "the love of money" is described as being "the root of all evil" (1 Timothy 6:10), cankering the souls of all who worship it more than they worship God. Yet industry and hard work, necessary to earn a livelihood for ourselves and our families, is honorable and expected of us by God. Money and wealth, and our attitude in accumulating it, can be a source of happiness or a source of sorrow or even damnation to us. It is important to understand where the difference lies.

> It's pretty hard to tell what does bring happiness. Poverty and wealth have both failed.
> ~Frank McKinney "Kin" Hubbard

Studies indicate that, in general, poor people are not as happy as people categorized as middle income. Certainly it's difficult to be happy when you are worried about where your family's next meal will come from. A certain amount of income is not only needed to provide the necessities of life, but to provide funds for serving missions, helping the poor, and providing donations to build up the kingdom of God on the earth. Money is also often needed to enable us to attend cultural events, to enroll in classes, or to participate in recreational or other activities from which we might find fulfillment and joy.

> Resolve not to be poor: whatever you have, spend less. Poverty is a great enemy to human happiness; it certainly destroys liberty, and it makes some virtues impracticable and others extremely difficult.
> ~Samuel Johnson

Studies further indicate that although those classified as middle income are generally happier than those classified as lower income, they are no less happy than those classified as upper income. In other words, once a person obtains sufficient income to take care of the basic necessities and a few niceties of life, additional income does little to provide additional happiness. On the next page is a graph that shows what the relationship between money and happiness is like:

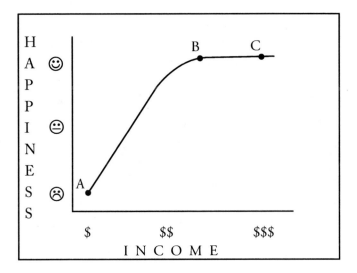

As depicted on this graph, the trick is to find point B, that point where happiness is maximized without the need to waste your precious time in the pursuit of additional, unnecessary wealth or things. For as playwright Neil Simon once stated, "Money brings some happiness. But after a certain point, it just brings more money."

Most people make the mistake of believing that having great wealth increases feelings of happiness. Consider, however, how many wealthy movie stars have unhappy marriages that result in divorce. Consider how many wealthy rock stars turn to alcohol or drugs to fight depression and misery. Great wealth can purchase some fleeting moments of worldly pleasure, but it cannot buy true happiness.

As noted by author Ernie Zelinski in his book *The Joy of Not Working*, pursuing and obtaining great wealth can actually have some negative affects on a person. For example, among the wealthy, personal relationships with friends and acquaintances can become strained or suffer. People are worried or afraid of losing their money or property from theft or through bad investments. With these added concerns, rather than becoming simpler, life becomes much more complicated and difficult. Taking care of and keeping tabs on all of the things you've accumulated with your wealth takes much of your time and becomes a hassle.

Zelinski further notes that besides the negative effects just listed, becoming rich often creates some significant character flaws in a person. For example, studies indicate that in the United States, more donating to the poor and needy is done by the poor and needy than by the rich. Pride, or a feeling of being above or better than others, also often becomes a problem among those who are wealthy.

Even among the not-quite-so-rich, the "wealthy wannabes", pursuing ever more wealth and material things can cause some serious problems in life. In his article "The Cost of Riches," Elder Lynn G. Robbins of the Seventy notes: "It has been said that a rich man doesn't own his things; rather, his things begin to own him."[2] He notes that "everything we buy consumes a part of our life"[3] For example, upgrading to a larger home "could cost an extra 5 to 10 years of life to purchase, depending on its cost. And if not 10 years of the father's life, then perhaps 10 years of the mother's life as a second wage earner."[4] We become a slave to our unnecessary possessions. They steal our time and our life from us, forcing us to leave home and to work longer and harder than we would otherwise need to. Elder Robbins continues:

> Joy is not in things; it is in us.
> ~Richard Wagner

> Benjamin Franklin said, "When you have bought one fine thing you must buy ten more, that your appearance may be all of a piece; ... 'tis easier to suppress the first desire than to satisfy all that follow it." This is especially true with today's tendency to purchase the biggest home possible, which requires not just 10 more "fine things" but hundreds to fill it. Families with barely affordable mortgage payments often turn to credit cards or a second wage earner to pay for these fine things. Too often the result is ever-increasing debt, manifest by record numbers of people filing for bankruptcy.[5]

In such circumstances, not only do we suffer, but our entire family suffers as a result. To one degree or another, our children are abandoned to raise themselves, often with tragic consequences. In our rush to obtain wealth, we often neglect, and sometimes forget, where our greatest treasure lies.

As one might well guess, to go past point B in accumulating wealth often results in an actual loss of happiness. Recent psychological studies confirm this fact. As reported in the *New York Times* on February 2, 1999, these studies indicate that "not only does having more things prove to be unfulfilling, but people for whom affluence is a priority in life tend to experience an unusual degree of anxiety and depression as well as a lower overall level of well-being."[6] The case of Josh is a prime example of this.

Josh was a happily married man who was employed as a middle manager by a large international corporation. He was making a great living earning $80,000 per year. Over time he became dissatisfied with his job, feeling that he could earn three times his salary each year if he owned his own company. With this greater income, he was certain he would be much happier.

One day he decided to take the plunge and set out on his own. Immediately his workdays went from nine to ten hours a day to twelve to fourteen hours per day. He often had to work weekends. The worries of keeping a new business going eventually gave him ulcers. He had little time for his family, but he kept telling himself that he was doing this for them and they should be grateful for all his sacrifices in their behalf. He had even less time for his Church callings.

Ten years of hard work finally paid off. He reached his goal. He was earning nearly $250,000 a year. However, during this same ten-year period, he was divorced from his wife and had become inactive in the Church. He had virtually no contact or relationship with his children, who never called or visited him (except, that is, to occasionally phone him to ask for money). As he sat alone in his

> The choice to serve God, worthily made, does not necessarily preclude a home or sufficient money or income, or things of this world which bring joy and happiness, but it does require that we must not turn away from God and the teachings of Jesus Christ while in the pursuit of our temporal needs.
>
> ~N. Eldon Tanner

fancy condominium, sipping on a glass of milk to ease his stomach problems, he thought back on his past. According to the world's definition, he was a success: he was financially well-to-do. Yet he knew that while his income had more than tripled, his feelings of peace and happiness were perhaps only a third of what they had once been. Was he really a success? Where had he gone wrong?

In his quest for wealth, Josh had been willing to sacrifice not just his time, but his health, his family, his happiness, and perhaps even his soul. For fame, fortune, or power others seem equally willing to sacrifice their integrity, their virtue, their God, and even their eternal salvation. What would you be willing to sacrifice for these temporary, worldly desires? Is it really worth it?

From Josh's story it becomes obvious to us that success in this life cannot simply be determined by the amount of worldly wealth someone has accumulated or the height of the position he has attained. Rather, the success of your life may more accurately be measured by how much true happiness you have experienced, how much spiritual growth you have achieved, and how many lives you have touched for good.

> It is neither wealth nor splendor, but tranquility and occupation, which give happiness.
> ~Thomas Jefferson

In the quest to apply this happiness principle in my own life, I took a long hard look at a part-time job I had. This job required me to spend every Friday evening away from home. I decided that the little extra money I earned from doing it was not worth the sacrifice of time away from my family; so I dropped it. In doing so I managed to coax another little bluebird onto my shoulder.

Money, and more importantly how we pursue it and our attitude toward it, can be either a blessing or a curse in our lives. It can help us achieve greater happiness or it can multiply our misery. Learn to use it wisely; allow it to help you increase, not decrease, your feelings of happiness.

Notes

1. Utah Business, Sept. 2000, 37, as quoted in Gordon B. Hinckley, "Great Shall Be the Peace of Thy Children," Ensign, Nov. 2000, 50.
2. Ensign, June 2003, 26.
3. Ibid.
4. Ibid.
5. Ibid., 27.
6. *New York Times*, February 2, 1999.

Happiness Principle #4:

Avoid excessive debt. If you're in it, get out of it

Professional counselors tell us that the number one cause of marital conflict is problems over finances, often related to excessive indebtedness. When it comes time to pay the bills each month and the money just isn't there, it is obviously going to cause stress and worry. Excessive stress and worry are both major happiness-killers.

Modern-day prophets have regularly warned of the danger of incurring excessive debt. In light of recent world events and circumstances, these prophetic warnings have become ever more loud and clear. As noted by President Gordon B. Hinckley:

> Life is fragile, peace is fragile, civilization itself is fragile. The economy is particularly vulnerable. We have been counseled again and again concerning self-reliance, concerning debt, concerning thrift. So many of our people are heavily in debt for things that are not entirely necessary. . . . I urge you as members of this Church to get free of debt where possible and to have a little laid aside against a rainy day. . . .
>
> I do not wish to sound negative, but I wish to remind you of the warnings of scripture and the teachings of the prophets which we have constantly before us.
>
> I cannot forget the great lesson of Pharaoh's dream of the fat and lean kine [cattle] and of the full and withered stalks of corn.[1]

Under present-day circumstances, it is more important than ever to get out of and stay out of debt. We are counseled to hold off on purchases until we can pay with cash. The few exceptions to this would be to purchase a home and perhaps an automobile. In some cases it may be necessary to go into debt to obtain an advanced education. Even in these few cases, however, one should make every effort to borrow as little as possible and pay it back as quickly as possible.

One of the real problems in the world today is that so many people just can't control their greediness. They are tricked into believing that material things in and of themselves will bring them instant happiness. As a result, they want everything they see, and they want it right now! This sickness is evident even among many Latter-day Saints. With greed out of control, too many of us are becoming financially overextended.

Many people suffer from what I call "Christmas Morning Syndrome." When our six children were young, Shelley and I would often spend several hundred dollars on toys for them at Christmas time. We enjoyed seeing the excitement on their faces as they opened their presents on Christmas morning. They would have so much fun playing with their new treasures that day. However, we soon discovered that by the end of the day they had already become tired of most of their toys. These would end up being thrown into the toy box, eventually sinking to the bottom, never to be resurrected again.

> Do not accustom yourself to consider debt only as an inconvenience; you will find it a calamity.
>
> ~Samuel Johnson

We became appalled at the vast waste of money involved in this yearly ritual. As years went by we tried to be wiser in our purchases, buying presents that we felt might be more practical, or at least hold the children's interest for a greater length of time.

I have known a number of grown adults who similarly suffer from "Christmas Morning Syndrome." They love to go shopping, receiving an adrenaline rush of excitement whenever they buy something new. Unfortunately, much like a child on Christmas morning, the high they receive from their most recent acquisition lasts for only a brief moment and then the excitement quickly fades. They must return quickly to the shopping mall once again in order to obtain their next fix. It's sad, but for many people buying things really does become an addiction. The excitement they experience from this practice lasts only for a brief moment because it is not real happiness.

Even if you don't have an addiction to shopping, you should stop walking into stores just to browse. The temptation to buy something you really don't need will always be there. Recently I had a friend at work describe how the day before he had driven twenty-five miles to a neighboring town to go to Wal-Mart. He made the trip specifically for the purpose of buying a particular tool that was required to finish a project he was working on. This was the sole purpose for the trip; there was nothing else he could think of that he needed. As he went through the checkout stand his purchases came to over eighty dollars. It was only after he arrived back at home, as he was putting things away, that he discovered he had forgotten to buy the needed tool.

Try an experiment: spend a whole month not purchasing anything in a store except your normal groceries and gasoline. When an item breaks, try repairing it instead of buying a new one. Make do with what you already have available to you. It's amazing how creative you can become. Break the buying habit!

Of course, it's not just lots of little purchases down at the local mall that can get us into debt or financial trouble. Huge homes and expensive toys lead to equally huge mortgages and costly credit card bills. This often leaves little money for obtaining the necessities of life, and virtually no money for enjoying activities that might actually provide some real satisfaction and happiness. It's a sad situation to be in, to say the least.

Now, think about your own situation. Are you in debt more than you should be? Is it causing you worry, stress, and perhaps some marital conflict? If so, this situation is definitely not adding to your feelings of peace and happiness. So, what can you do to get your finances under control and start feeling better? Here are a few suggestions:

1. If you're not one already, become a full-tithe payer. You need the "windows of heaven" opened to you, so that you can receive the blessings that God has promised to all tithe payers.

2. Put together a reasonable personal budget and financial plan that will help you achieve both your short-term and long-term financial goals. If you are married, work as a couple on a budget and financial plan that you both agree on. Write down and keep a log of all your purchases so you can see where your money is being spent. Knowing that you will have to record what you are spending your money on will cause you to carefully consider what you are buying.

3. Is your house providing you less happiness than your mortgage payment is providing grief? If you were in a smaller house with a smaller mortgage payment, would it reduce your worries and free up more money to enjoy additional happiness-producing activities? Could you quit your second job and have more time to enjoy with your family? Remember that happiness is your number one goal. What circumstances will maximize it?

4. If monthly installment payments are killing you, leaving you little money for even the basic necessities, would you be better off to consolidate your bills into one loan with a lower monthly payment? Be careful—only consider this if your finances are really in a mess and you are certain you can change the buying habits that got you into this predicament in the first place. Studies indicate that nearly 85 percent of those who take out a loan to consolidate their debts have fallen back into debt within three years, plus still have the earlier loan to pay off.

5. Set up a plan to pay off your debts. Make all your regular monthly payments and then with any extra money you have left over, pay extra on your smallest debt, preferably the one with the highest interest rate. After it has been paid off, use the money you were previously using to make payments on this debt toward paying off the next smallest debt. As each debt is paid, continue using the money you free up to pay off the next one. This will have a "snowball" effect because each month you will have more money available to use toward debt reduction.

By ridding yourself of the smallest debts first, you will feel like you are making progress and will remain motivated to stick with your plan.

6. Look for ways to cut costs in your monthly expenses such as on utilities, food, and insurance bills. There are some great books you can check out at your local library that can teach you how to be a "cheapskate" or "tightwad." Or do a Google search on "frugal living." Figure out how you can apply some of the principles these books and websites describe.

7. Cut up all your credit cards except for one that you can use for emergencies when on trips. Drop the limit on this card down to about $2,000. That way there is no way you can ever run up a credit card debt of $5,000 or $10,000 like you may have in the past. This will force you to stay in control.

8. Create peace of mind through building some financial security for yourself. Obtain adequate medical and life insurance. Work on building up some savings for retirement and emergencies. Work toward obtaining a year's supply of food storage and at least three months' worth of emergency cash savings.

During our married life together, at one time or another Shelley and I have had to implement nearly all of these techniques. With recent counsel coming from the prophets, we have chosen to delay some vacation plans and desired purchases this year and instead have made a focused effort to pay off our car, lower our insurance premiums, and increase our savings and food storage. With obedience comes blessings and we are already reaping good feelings of peace and security from our efforts.

Constantly worrying about money matters can be a major source of unhappiness in one's life. As you work toward getting your finances under control, you are bound to find your feelings of peace and happiness on the rise.

Notes
1. Gordon B. Hinckley, Ensign, Nov. 2001, 73.

Happiness Principle #5:

Enjoy the blessings of work

Brigham Young once stated: "Each will find that happiness in this world mainly depends on the work he does, and the way in which he does it." Work gives purpose to life. It gives us a reason to get up in the morning. To some degree it defines who we are and serves as an outlet for our creative efforts. These are just a few of the benefits of work in our lives.

For those of us who work for a living, even the most mundane, repetitive, and boring job can bring far more happiness than having no job at all. Studies show that men who have been out of work for several months commonly experience varying degrees of boredom, discouragement, and depression. They are anything but happy. So count yourself fortunate just to have a job, even if it isn't quite as exciting, meaningful, or fulfilling as you would like it to be.

> Happiness does not come from doing easy work but from the afterglow of satisfaction that comes after the achievement of a difficult task that demanded our best.
> ~Theodore I. Rubin

If you are fortunate enough to actually enjoy the job that you do, so much the better, and what a blessing in your life! If you don't, what could you do to make it more enjoyable? Imagine that you are part-owner of the company. Can you discover ways to save the company money? Ways to increase productivity or sales? Ways to work more efficiently in your particular position? Look for some aspect of your job that challenges your ingenuity and creative abilities.

Of course, the best way to achieve happiness in your work is to choose and enthusiastically pursue a career that appeals to you. In such a job or career you feel a sense of purpose and achievement. To you, it is not work at all!

If you are not satisfied with your current employment, perhaps a more desirable, fulfilling job would pay less but would increase your feelings of happiness. Might it be worth the change? If so, make a plan of action. Maybe you will first need to take some night classes to learn more about a particular field, start your new career as a part-time business owner, or reduce some personal debts so that you can still live comfortably on less income. You spend over half your waking hours doing some type of work. So, do whatever it takes to make happiness an integral part of your work life.

> To love what you do and feel that it matters—how could anything be more fun?
>
> ~Katharine Graham

Four Ways to Make the Work You Do More Fulfilling and Joyful

We work not only at the office, factory, farm, or store to secure a livelihood, but we also perform work at home, at church, and at many other places. Since we spend so much of each day working, it is important to understand how we can increase and even maximize the happiness we experience from the work that we do.

There are some powerful principles each of us can utilize that will turn work into joy. For the sake of brevity, I will describe just four of these principles here. Be aware that the more of these principles you incorporate into your own work life—whether on the job, at home, at church, or wherever—the more fulfillment and happiness you will feel.

The first two work-related happiness principles are summarized by Laurence G. Boldt in his book *How to Find the Work You Love*:

> To the extent that your work takes into account the needs of the world, it will be meaningful; to the extent that through it you express your unique talents, it will be joyful.[1]

Principle #1: Pursue work that is worthwhile, fulfilling, and meaningful.

Certain jobs are, by nature, more fulfilling than others. If in your work you sense that you are blessing the lives of others, your feelings of fulfillment and joy will be enhanced. For example, a doctor can experience happiness knowing that he is using his knowledge and skills to relieve pain and suffering in his patients. An artist feels deep satisfaction in creating a beautiful painting that will be enjoyed by all who see it. And a janitor can experience a good feeling knowing that others will enjoy a clean, pleasant work place as a result of his hard work. In each case, there is a sense that one's work benefits someone else.

Sally is a stay-at-home mom. She thinks she has the best job in the world: raising five great kids to be responsible, mature adults. Her goal is to raise children that love God. She seeks for each child to possess a burning testimony of the truthfulness of the restored Church and gospel of Jesus Christ. What greater and more meaningful work can one find than that of spending one's life in serving and saving one's own offspring? It is the same work that God does, and in which He finds His greatest joy and fulfillment. (See Moses 1:39.)

Principle #2: Use your unique talents in the work that you do.

Matching your talents, interests, and skills with the work you do will definitely make your work more satisfying and joyful. If you are shy or introverted, you should probably not be a car salesman. On the other hand, if you are outgoing and extroverted, you would probably not be happy as an accountant in a one-man office. Does your personality match your job? What unique talents or interests do you have? If you were a millionaire and were working just for the fun of it, what job or profession would you choose? Thoughtfully answering this question might provide you with some direction as to where to find the greatest fulfillment in pursuing a career.

Sally from the previous example has a nurturing personality. Even as a young child her favorite activity was playing mother to her host of dolls. During her lifetime she has never lost her deep love for motherhood, and her talents and abilities all seem to revolve around it.

Principle #3: Love what you do . . . and have fun doing it!

Thomas Edison said: "I never did a day's work in my life. It has all been fun."[2] That could sum up Sally's life experience also. She has the unique ability of turning work into fun.

Sally loves being at home and finds her greatest fulfillment there. Certainly there are certain aspects of being a homemaker that aren't all that exciting: ironing clothes, doing the laundry, and washing dishes, to name just a few. But she feels that these few negatives are more than offset by so many other positive aspects of working at home.

There is never a dull moment around her house when she is home. One of her greatest joys is planning the weekly family activity or party. During the winter this might consist of a beach party in the living room, complete with swimwear, balloon volleyball, Beach Boy music, a glass of cool lemonade to sip on, and assorted games. Or it might entail a winter campout where the children help Dad to pitch their eight-man tent in the middle of the family room. The family might then roast hot dogs and marshmallows in the fireplace, and tell spooky stories while lying in the dark in their sleeping bags.

During holiday seasons things get even more bizarre at Sally's house. She goes absolutely wild directing all the crazy fun. She loves her job as activity director of her family and pursues it with a passion. As a result, family members have shared so many great memories together and everyone has been greatly blessed.

Principle #4: Use your creativity to build something special.

Some of the most fulfilling and enjoyable work one can do involves building or creating something. Such work taps into one's creative abilities. This may involve working on an actual structure, such as building a house or remodeling the kitchen. It may include landscaping and planting a beautiful flower garden or creating a work of art. A sense of creation can likewise be felt in planning and building a personal business or in working to create a more positive, team-oriented attitude among the employees of a business organization. There are many different ways we can use our creative abilities in the work that we do. I personally have experienced much happiness and fulfillment just by using my creative powers to write this book. When we create something good, there always follows a sense of accomplishment, fulfillment, and joy.

I would venture to guess that the Creator Himself had a great deal of enjoyment, and perhaps even some fun, while creating and organizing this earth along with all the various plants and animals He placed upon it. There must have been a feeling of great satisfaction and joy when He looked upon His finished masterpiece of creation and pronounced it "good" (Genesis 1:31).

Sally similarly feels a sense of creation in working with her children. Not only was she a partner with God in creating each of their physical bodies and mortal lives, but she uses her God-given creative abilities to help build character in each one. As she watches her children grow and make wise and righteous choices, there is a good feeling in her heart and a sense of accomplishment that all her hard work is paying off. In her partnership with God, there is a sense of joy that accompanies the work of creating faithful sons and daughters of God.

So, what is the bottom line in our discussion on work? Find joy in the work you do. Work can, and should, be one of the greatest sources of happiness in your life.

Notes

1. Laurence G. Boldt, *How to Find the Work You Love* (New York, New York: Penguin Group, 1996), 9.
2. equotes.wetpaint.com/page/Thomas+Edison+Quotes?t-anon.

Now take a moment to ponder and really consider the first five happiness principles you have just been taught. Are you already living all of them? Do you have all five little bluebirds sitting on your shoulders? If not, which of these five principles, if you were to begin to fully apply it, would have the greatest immediate impact in increasing your personal happiness? What specific steps can you take to begin implementing this principle in your life today?

Part Three:

A Happier Life Through Greater Physical Well-Being

Happiness Principle #6:

Keep your physical body healthy and happy

It is nearly impossible to feel really happy when you feel yucky and sick. Of course, none of us can expect to travel through life without some bouts with illness, but considering the affect that bad health has on our happiness, we should take all the steps necessary to maximize our health and prevent illness. In our golden years we will be happy that we did. What a tragedy it would be to work your whole life, looking forward to the day you can finally retire, and then not have the necessary health to do all the things you were looking forward to doing.

In her wonderful little book, *365 Health and Happiness Boosters,* author M. J. Ryan, notes a national happiness survey conducted by Harvard University. In the survey, 46 percent of those questioned said that the greatest source of happiness is "good health." It received the highest score on the survey. Although most of us take good health for granted, we should be aware of the negative affect it can have on our happiness if suddenly we no longer enjoy it.

> Happiness lies, first of all, in health.
> ~George William Curtis

While we should do all that we can to maintain our good health, we should also recognize that even if we do become sick or disabled, all is not lost. A positive attitude can make a tremendous difference. Studies indicate that those who accept their physical shortcomings are far happier than those who mope around feeling sorry for themselves.

43

There are three areas to focus on in improving one's physical health: diet, exercise, and rest. How are you doing in each area? Could you improve your diet by eating fewer fatty and sugary foods and eating more whole grains, fruits, and vegetables? Are you conscious of any unhealthy eating habits you have such as regularly stuffing yourself at the dinner table? Do you drink plenty of water each day? Do you avoid eating within two hours before going to bed? What about rest? Are you regularly getting enough sleep (but not too much)? And finally, what about exercise? Do you have a regular program? If not, I'll bet I know why. As M. J. Ryan notes:

> Ugh! I hate exercise, and frankly I usually feel too tired to do it (I'm not alone—a study by Penn State discovered that fatigue is the reason given by 70 percent of people who fail to exercise regularly). But the truth is that exercise is just what we need to feel good—increased blood flow from exercise oxygenates the body and makes you feel more energized.[1]

Ironic, isn't it? We don't have enough energy to exercise, and yet it's exercise that will increase our energy!

Besides increasing our energy level and zest for life, regular exercise provides us with many other benefits. Studies show that people who regularly exercise have fewer heart attacks; sleep better; think more clearly; are better able to manage stress; have higher "good" cholesterol; have less back pain; are less likely to be overweight (a significant problem in our society today); have improved heart, lung, and digestive functioning; look, feel, and work better; and live longer and healthier lives. It's really a no-brainer; with so many obvious benefits, *everyone* needs to be involved in a regular exercise program.

> A healthy body is the guest-chamber of the soul; a sick, its prison.
> ~Francis Bacon

Some people have trouble going to sleep at night, tossing and turning as they relive the happenings of the day or worry about the demands of the next. Does this happen to you? Calm down and forget about your worries before going to bed by spending some time reading the scriptures, meditating, and praying. Get life back in perspective and take time to count your blessings. This should become a nightly ritual for you.

If you still have problems sleeping, try turning on a fan, playing some soft music (the kind with the sound of the ocean or a running stream in the background), or running a humidifier in your bedroom. The sound of running water or a humming sound can have a soothing effect that will help you sleep more soundly. If necessary visit a doctor, or even better, visit the Lord with your problem. Don't learn to live with insomnia—learn how to overcome it. If you are constantly tired, you are too tired to be happy.

> Health is like money, we never have a true idea of its value until we lose it.
> ~Josh Billings

As we grow older our metabolism slows down and we tend to gain weight. I am a little over six feet tall, and for most of my early married years I weighed about 180 pounds, which was just right for me. In my late forties I put on ten pounds and in my early fifties, I put on still another ten pounds. At one point in time I managed to reach a nice, plump 213 pounds. I remember looking at a photo of myself standing in front of the Salt Lake Temple following my oldest daughter, Charity's, wedding. I looked so terrible, and physically felt so terrible, that I determined then and there that if I wanted to be healthy and happy right then, as well as in my later years, I needed to work to lose some weight right away.

During the ensuing months, through much sweat and tears, I managed to get back down to around 190 pounds. Perhaps you are wondering why I didn't just keep going and get down to my original 180 pounds. Well, when I reached 190 pounds I seemed to hit one of those set points beyond which it is extremely difficult to lose more weight. Although I knew that I would look and feel even better if I were to get all the way back down to 180 pounds, quite frankly I questioned if it was worth the effort. I asked myself, "What will make me happiest?" Obviously, I would be

> So many people spend their health gaining wealth, and then have to spend their wealth to regain their health.
> ~A. J. Reb Materi

happier weighing 180 than 190. But, with my slower metabolism, I would also have to starve and torture myself, working out an extra half hour a day for the rest of my life, to be able to stay there. This would have decreased my feelings of happiness. In the process of losing the extra ten pounds, I would have been both adding to my happiness and subtracting from my happiness. Thus, my net gain in increased happiness for the effort would be zero. Obviously, that half hour of time could be better spent on other activities providing me a much higher rate of return in happiness. So, I worked out a compromise, or a "happy medium." I decided to stay at 190. Although 190 isn't as good as 180, it is far better than 213!

> Doctors are always working to preserve our health and cooks to destroy it, but the latter are the more often successful.
>
> ~Denis Diderot

I feel that my final decision to stay at 190 was quite a mature decision on my part. It came only after I looked at myself closely in the mirror. Observing the wrinkles in my face, my sagging chin, and the streaks of silver in my hair, it suddenly dawned on me that in this lifetime I would probably never look like a twenty-year-old again. This was a truly shocking revelation at the time, but I have bravely learned to live with it.

Today, I generally try to eat right, but the truth is I still allow myself the pleasure of an occasional slice or two of apple pie or pizza. After all, I'm only going to live once and my taste buds deserve a little joy in life too, don't they? I am certain that God gave us taste buds so we could better enjoy life.

Remember that by eating right, exercising regularly, and getting sufficient rest, you can reduce stress, increase energy, build up your immune system, and maintain a properly functioning, healthy body. Such a body is absolutely essential if you hope to fully participate in all of those happiness-producing activities that you listed in Happiness Principle 1. So do it! Make the effort to be healthy and be happy.

Notes

1. M. J. Ryan, *365 Health and Happiness Boosters*, 98.

Happiness Principle #7:

Maintain a clean, organized, beautiful, peaceful living environment

The physical environment we live in can have a significant effect on how we feel. Our surroundings can cause us to feel either negative emotions, such as fear, stress, sadness, and depression, or positive emotions, such as peace, tranquility, contentment, and joy. We usually feel more cheerful on a bright, sunny day than we do on a gloomy, rainy day. I feel more at peace while sitting in the temple than I do while sitting in a car driving in noisy rush-hour traffic in downtown Chicago. I feel far better strolling through a beautifully manicured flower garden and arboretum than I feel when strolling through a city slum filled with vacant and vandalized buildings.

Apply this same positive-emotion-producing principle to your home: Clean it and brighten it to create a peaceful, happy atmosphere. There are many simple ways to change your home's atmosphere. Could some wallpaper or a coat of paint help? Plants and flowers? Pictures of the Savior and a temple on the walls? Soft music playing in the background? Some

> Love of beauty is Taste. The creation of beauty is Art.
> ~Ralph Waldo Emerson

fragrant potpourri, candles, or air fresheners to stimulate the sense of smell? Extra lights to brighten those dark rooms? Next to the temple, your home should be the place where you feel your best.

There are significant psychological benefits associated with the proper use of music and lighting and the sight of beautiful objects and landscapes. The right kind of music, carefully chosen, can create within us moods and feelings of reverence, worship, peace, tranquility, cheerfulness, and joy. Lighting is also significant. Does your home contain enough of this precious commodity?

My eldest son, Tad, served his mission in Norway. Norwegians, as a whole, are a very happy people. This may be partially because they live in such beautiful surroundings with magnificent mountains, valleys, and fjords. Tad spent about seven months of his mission in a city that was north of the Arctic Circle. During nearly three months of his stay there, he never saw the sun. With the exception of a few minutes of twilight in the early morning, it was dark nearly twenty-four hours a day. He can attest to the fact that during these months of darkness, the people were far less friendly and less likely to invite the missionaries into their homes than they were during those months when the sun shone every day. No question about it, living in darkness can lead to grumpiness and even depression.

> Think of all the beauty that's still left in and around you and be happy!
>
> ~Anne Frank

Our feelings of happiness (or grouchiness) are similarly affected by the physical beauty (or ugliness) of our surroundings. This is perhaps why Brigham Young gave the following counsel:

> Let the husband make an improvement upon his kitchen and pantry and upon his bedrooms for the benefit of the family, and improve his gardens, walks, etc., beautifying your habitations and their surroundings, making pavements and planting shade trees....
>
> It is your right, wives, to ask your husbands to set out beautiful shade and fruit trees, and to get you some vines and flowers with which to adorn the outside of your dwellings; and if your husbands have not the time, get them yourselves and plant them out. Some, perhaps, will say, "Oh, I have nothing but a log house, and it is not worth that." Yes; it is worth it. Whitewash and plaster it up, and get vines to run over the door, so that

everybody who passes will say, "What a lovely little cottage!" This is your privilege and I wish you to exercise yourselves in your own rights. . . .

Beautify your gardens, your houses, your farms; beautify the city. This will make us happy, and produce plenty.[1]

Each spring, after a long winter spent mainly indoors, Gary and Betty are eager to get outside and start making improvements on their house and yard. Recently they completed a landscaping project near the back of their property on a piece of ground that had previously been a weed patch surrounding a lone apricot tree. They rolled up their sleeves and went to work transforming this barren spot into a terraced garden spot, dressed with flowers, bushes, and a patio area. They added a sunken fire pit where they sit as a family on cool summer evenings roasting marshmallows or just staring at the fire and visiting. This project increased their happiness in four ways:

1. The yard is now more beautiful, which increases their feelings of peace and happiness whenever they venture into the backyard to enjoy the outdoors.

2. They said it was fun to use their creative abilities in designing the flower beds and planting the bushes and flowers. Each time they gaze upon this beautiful section of their yard, they feel a sense of accomplishment and satisfaction in knowing that together they created and built this wonderful little masterpiece of art through their own mental and physical hard work.

3. Gary no longer has to spend twenty minutes every other week all summer long digging weeds out of this area. Before planting the bushes and flowers, they covered much of the area in plastic and tree bark thus preventing weeds from growing. A built-in sprinkler makes watering the area simple. He has thus eliminated forever from his life a job that he never enjoyed.

4. The area under the apricot tree is now a perfect home for Gary's hammock. With the extra time he now has (from not having to pull all of those ugly weeds) he can spend more time relaxing in the hammock while reading a good book, napping,

or simply gazing at the clouds and daydreaming. Ah, the good life! Yes, they are saving time and have simplified their lives.

So do what President Young said—beautify your home and the grounds surrounding it. Even if it's small in size, you can make your home a beautiful palace and a peaceful sanctuary, a heaven on earth that will bless the lives of all who live there.

Notes

1. John A. Widtsoe, ed., *Discourses of Brigham Young* (Salt Lake City, Utah: Bookcraft, 1954), 198, 200, 302.

Happiness Principle #8:

Live an active, not a passive life

All studies on the subject indicate that people who live an active life are much happier than people who live a passive life. This is not to say that all passive activities are bad. Sometimes you need to totally relax and imitate a vegetable. In years past, about once a month our family would gather around the television to watch a good video and munch on some popcorn. During the fall I would regularly take my sons over to a friend's house to watch the cable broadcasts of BYU football games. Although with as much yelling, screaming, and jumping up and down as they did, for my boys this was not really a passive activity.

While watching a good movie once in a while is both enjoyable and relaxing, as a general rule people who spend too much time in front of the television set each day often become lethargic and bored with life. This can lead to feelings of sadness and even depression. If this describes you, you need to turn off the TV, get off the couch, and start living! Attend a class, develop a talent, enjoy a hobby, visit a friend, read a good book, do some yard work, go exercise, or participate in

> Twenty years from now you will be more disappointed by the things that you didn't do than by the things you did. So throw off the bowlines. Sail away from the safe harbor. Catch the trade winds in your sail. Explore. Dream. Discover.
>
> ~Mark Twain

sports. Don't expect happiness to come searching for you. Go out and find where all those little bluebirds are hiding.

In his book *The Conquest of Happiness* (1930), author Bertrand

Russell describes happiness as the possession of zest. He states that "what hunger is in relation to food, zest is in relation to life."[1] According to Russell, a person with zest might be compared to a very hungry person who sits down at the dinner table anxious to eat. This person appreciates and savors each bite he takes and eats heartily until he is completely full. Zest is enjoying life fully because we find it interesting and are hungry for it. It is an enthusiasm for a variety of pursuits in life.

> People must learn to gather adventures and experiences rather than things and possessions. Possessions will burden you, but adventures are memories which will enrich your soul and they will last forever.
> ~Alfred A. Montapert

Russell provides several more illustrations of zest, comparing those who do and who don't possess this happiness-producing trait. For example, he finds that those without zest often find others they meet to be boring. People with zest, however, find other people interesting and want to get to know them better. As another example, Russell states,

> Take again such a matter as travel; some men will travel through many countries, going always to the best hotels, eating exactly the same food as they would eat at home, meeting the same idle rich whom they would meet at home, conversing on the same topics upon which they converse at their own dinner table. When they return, their only feeling is one of relief at having done with the boredom of expensive locomotion. Other men wherever they go see what is characteristic, make the acquaintance of people who typify the locality, observe whatever is of interest either historically or socially, eat the food of the country, learn its manners and its language, and come home with a new stock of pleasant thoughts for winter evenings.
>
> In all these different situations the man who has the zest for life has the advantage over the man who has none.[2]

Zest includes a curiosity for our surroundings and a desire to explore and to experience life to its fullest.

Now, what about you? Are you in a rut? If life's routine is getting too repetitive and boring for you, find something new to be passionate about. Experience a little zest! Set a goal or two for yourself. For example, you may determine that it's finally time to lose those twenty extra pounds you've been carrying around for so long. Get

> Happiness consists in activity: such is the constitution of our nature: it is a running stream, and not a stagnant pool.
> ~J. M. Good.

serious and get passionate about losing them. Or perhaps you have a problem with low energy. Set a goal to become an expert on its causes and how to change it. Learn what to eat and drink, what exercises to perform, and what other actions you can employ that will be most effective in increasing your lagging energy. Apply what you've learned, and then share with others what you have discovered.

Make a list of twelve classic novels or historical fiction novels, such as Charles Dickens's *David Copperfield* or Gerald Lund's *The Work and the Glory*, and read one volume a month for a year. Set a goal to turn your front yard into lovely "temple grounds" with beautiful flower beds all around. Remodel your kitchen or family room, doing all the work yourself. Develop a new talent. Begin a new hobby. Or, become a big brother or big sister to a disadvantaged child. Thoughtfully choose whatever goal you wish and

> There is no pleasure in having nothing to do; the fun is in having lots to do and not doing it.
> ~John W. Rapa

then jump into it with both feet, allowing the journey to its achievement to create a greater love for life within you.

If you live an active, zestful life, you won't become like so many people who, a few months after retiring from their job, travel back to the workplace. Why do they do so? Because they don't know what to do with all the free time they now have. They are bored to death! They have developed so few interests during their lifetime, and have so little zest, that they can't keep themselves occupied and happy for a day, let alone the remainder of their lives.

If you haven't acquired a variety of interests, talents, and an active lifestyle during your younger and middle-aged years, it's not likely that you will do so during your retirement years. So if you want to be happy your entire life, learn how to really enjoy and fully live life. Stay active and experience zest!

Notes

1. Bertrand Russell, *The Conquest of Happiness* (New York: Liveright Publishing Corporation, 1930), 163.
2. Ibid.

Part Four:

A Happier Life Through Greater Social Well-Being

Happiness Principle #9:

Work toward a celestial marriage

Our single years can and should be very happy years. We can live these years zestfully, filling them with meaningful, fulfilling, growing experiences and wonderful friendships. During these years, with the exception of marriage and children, all of the happiness principles discussed in this book can be fully applied in our lives.

As Latter-day Saints we know that the crowning ordinance of the gospel is temple marriage. While we are single we should strive to keep ourselves clean and worthy of being joined with an eternal companion in the House of the Lord. We may find our eternal companion relatively early in this life, later in life, or perhaps not until after we have died. The Lord has made certain that no child of His who proves worthy and is desirous of this blessing will ever be denied it. No matter when this crowning ordinance might take place in our lives, either in this life or the next, while we are single we should be actively engaged in developing a virtuous character and becoming the kindest, most unselfish, and ultimately the most wonderful marriage partner we can be.

> A truly happy marriage is one in which a woman gives the best years of her life to the man who made them the best.
>
> ~Author unknown

Studies by social scientists indicate that married people describe themselves as being happier and more fulfilled than do those who are single. The happiest marriages are those in which both partners are not only close as a couple, but each partner also allows and even encourages the growth of his or her spouse as an individual.

God created man and woman to complement one another. The scriptures teach that when a couple is joined in marriage, they become "one flesh" (Genesis 2:24). It would logically follow then that as a single entity, each individual is less than one, meaning that as an individual, one is not fully complete.

God has revealed in our day that in eternity the highest degree of happiness in the celestial kingdom will only be enjoyed by married couples. If marriage is to eventually become one of the greatest sources of happiness in eternity, it would seem logical to assume it can be, and should be, one of the greatest sources of happiness in this life also.

Just as marriage can be a major source of happiness and fulfillment, so also can it be a major source of misery. Pride and selfishness can turn a marriage sour. A domineering and controlling husband, much like a communist dictator, can destroy his wife's freedom, thus restricting her ability to pursue happiness-producing activities. On the other hand, a constantly nagging and critical wife can drive her husband crazy or make him utterly miserable. Since marriage can become either a major source of happiness or a major source of misery, we should do all that we can to ensure that it becomes the former and not the latter.

God has placed within man and woman a natural attraction for one another—an internal magnet you might say. Once one has found a compatible companion, this attraction may ultimately lead to marriage. After the first few months of marriage, when some of the initial romantic feelings have begun to fade a little and the realities of life have begun to set in, then comes the true test of a marriage. Although it does take some work, a celestial marriage filled with true friendship, love, and happiness can begin to form at this point in time if both partners really desire it.

> Do not think that you can make a girl lovely if you do not make her happy.
> ~John Ruskin

The secret to a happy, celestial marriage is actually quite simple; it is two-fold. First, it involves each partner striving to live as

Christlike a life as he or she possibly can. The attributes of the Savior include kindness, honesty, patience, compassion, pure love, service to others, humility, unselfishness, faithfulness, loyalty, and many other similar noble traits of a completely righteous being. One cannot help but see that it would be quite easy to love a person who possessed such qualities. If feelings of love once brought a couple together but have since faded, then such feelings can come to life again by both partners following the example of the Savior through living a life of righteousness.

> Whatever woman may cast her lot with mine, should any ever do so, it is my intention to do all in my power to make her happy and contented; and there is nothing I can imagine that would make me more unhappy than to fail in the effort.
>
> ~Abraham Lincoln

Of course we must be patient with our partners as well as ourselves. Perfection does not come quickly; it is generally quite a slow process. (We shall speak more of what is involved in this perfecting process in a later chapter.) As we work at changing for the better, we should not attempt to control the actions or growth of our partner. We can lovingly encourage, or offer advice if requested, but ultimately each person is responsible for his own growth and improvement. To be most effective, the desire to change and improve must ultimately come from internal sources, not external. As your desire to grow and to become more Christlike turns to reality, you will find yourself becoming both more lovable and more able to love, and your marriage will improve tremendously because of it.

The second part of this two-fold secret to a happy marriage is captured and summarized by Edward George Bulwer-Lytton: "There is one way of attaining what we may term, if not utter, at least mortal happiness; it is by a sincere and unrelaxing activity for the happiness of others."[1]

Nowhere is this truth more applicable than in a marriage relationship. No other mortal on earth currently holds more ability and power to increase your feelings of happiness than does your spouse. As you actively work for your partner's fulfillment and happiness, you ensure an increase of your own. In nearly all cases, what you give

> The thing that counts most
> in the pursuit of happiness
> is choosing the right
> traveling companion.
> ~Adrian Anderson

will eventually be returned. Kindness begets kindness, respect begets respect, courtesy begets courtesy, love begets love. For the sake of your own happiness, no other relationship on earth is more important for you to nurture and strengthen than that of your own marriage. So go to work doing all in your power to ensure the happiness of your eternal companion, and see if you don't find your own feelings of happiness suddenly on the rise.

Notes

1. www.madwed.com/quotes/Quotations/Stories/Habits_Happiness/
body_habits_happiness.html

Happiness Principle #10:

Nourish a happy family life

Wise are the words of the psalmist who wrote, "Lo, children are an heritage of the Lord: and the fruit of the womb is his reward. As arrows are in the hand of a mighty man; so are children of the youth. Happy is the man that hath his quiver full of them" (Psalm 127:3–5).

Home and family life can be, and should be, one of the greatest sources of happiness we can ever tap into. Making the effort to develop close, loving relationships with those we care about most should be among our highest priorities. Our investment of quality time with our family is well worth it. It provides a rate of return in love and joy that far exceeds that which any stock, bond, or business deal could ever give us.

Several years ago, while speaking at a BYU Education Week, a medical doctor spoke on this subject. He told a little story about his own family that illustrates this point. He related how one summer, about a year earlier, he had taken his family on a two-week vacation to Europe. As you can imagine, he spent thousands of dollars to provide this once-in-a-lifetime opportunity for his wife and ten children.

On the first day of school the following September, this doctor's eight-year-old son was asked to write a paper on what his favorite, most exciting event of the previous summer had been. You would think that the boy would

> A happy family is but an earlier heaven.
>
> ~Robert Browning

have written all about his tour of Europe. But no. Instead he wrote about the Friday night that his dad had come home from work and, on the spur of the moment, decided to take he and his brother on an overnight campout and fishing trip. Now that was something special, something fantastic: a special time with Dad that he would always remember.

> The happiest moments of my life have been the few which I have passed at home in the bosom of my family.
> ~Thomas Jefferson

The trip to Europe had cost the doctor perhaps ten thousand dollars or more. The fishing trip had cost him only about ten dollars. Yet the fishing trip was of far greater value to the boy. Why? Because of the quality one-on-one time he got to spend with his dad. To this eight-year-old boy, that time alone was worth more than all the money in the world.

Provide Your Children with Both Soft Love and Tough Love

In hopes of winning a child's love and becoming their "best friend," many parents provide their children with little or no discipline. This is why so many schools today are filled with children who have no respect for adults or rules. Having never learned to obey their parents, children never learn to obey their teachers. What is even worse, having never learned respect for adults or any form of authority, children never learn to obey God.

Although it is not always easy, parents need to set family rules and then enforce them. When children misbehave, they need to be corrected. If parents truly love their children they must teach them to be obedient. To do so they sometimes have to administer discipline or tough love.

While many parents make the mistake of providing little or no discipline, at the other end of the spectrum are those parents who are constantly disciplining their children. These children grow up feeling like they can do nothing right. As they grow older, eventually they will rebel against their parents and, unfortunately, will likely rebel against God also.

To be effective as parents, we need to function somewhere in the middle of these two extremes. We can prevent rebellion and still be our child's best friend if we offset the occasional tough love with even larger doses of soft love.

Some describe the relationship between a parent and a child in terms of an emotional bank account. Certainly no one likes to be disciplined; when we punish a child for disobedience, a certain amount of positive emotion is withdrawn from this account. What we as parents need to ensure is that more deposits are going into this account than withdrawals are being taken out.

We make deposits whenever we spend quality time together, show sincere interest, and let each of our children know that we truly love and care about him. By working together and playing together, we grow close to one another. Then children come to obey their parents, not out of the fear of being punished, but because they love them. Eventually they learn to obey God for the same reason.

When Children Rebel

Even the best parents sometimes have a child that is prone to rebellion. No matter how much love they are shown, for some reason the teachings of the gospel just don't seem to sink in. Much to the sorrow of their parents, these children are determined to seek happiness in all the wrong places.

> The first duty to children is to make them happy. If you have not made them so, you have wronged them. No other good they may get can make up for that.
>
> ~Charles Buxton

When faced with such a challenge, parents need to remember two things. First, never give up on your children. Continue to love them and pray for them. Although you may not approve of their behavior, do not push them farther away by constantly criticizing them. They definitely need to know that you are unhappy with their decisions, but don't spend a lot of time harping on it. Make sure you keep your relationship positive. It's the best hope you have of eventually reaching them.

Second, although sorrow fills the heart of any righteous parent who has a rebellious child, don't let this overcome the feelings of happiness you can and should be feeling in your life. Remember that not even Heavenly Father was able to save all of His children. Recognize the good that you have done in your child's life. As Stephen E. Robinson explains:

> Do you have troubled or unfaithful children? Then picture the following scene. I can't prove it represents true doctrine, but I dearly believe it does. Suppose the Father brings you a little baby spirit and says, "This child is going to have more problems than most in mortality, but I know that if she is raised in your home she will rise higher and go farther than if she were anywhere else. Will you take her and love her and maximize her potential? It will be hard, because she's not going to get straight A's, and she won't win any awards. There will be things she can't overcome, and there will at times be great pain for you. But she is my baby, and she is precious to me, and I know she will go farther and rise higher with you for her parents than with anyone else. Won't you please take her and love her as I do?"[1]

Perhaps, no matter how much you desire it, this child will never qualify for exaltation in the celestial kingdom. But very likely this child, perhaps telestial in nature, will rise to receive a far greater eternal reward than he would have otherwise, simply because he grew up in your wonderful home. One day this child will thank you for the blessings you brought into his life. Be happy and grateful that you had the opportunity to do so.

> A man travels the world over in search of what he needs, and returns home to find it.
> ~George Moore

Yes, there can be great challenges in parenting and in maintaining family harmony and closeness. Overcoming these challenges is not always easy. But the rewards in increased happiness and love make it worth the effort.

Notes

1. Robinson, Stephen E., *Following Christ* (Salt Lake City, Utah: Deseret Book Company, 2004), 146.

Now, take a moment to ponder and really consider happiness principles six through ten that you have just been taught. Are you already living all of them? Look over and down at your shoulders. How many of these five little bluebirds can you see currently sitting there? Which of these five principles would have the greatest immediate impact toward increasing your feelings of personal happiness if you were to begin to fully apply it in your life? What goals can you set for yourself and what specific steps can you take to begin implementing this principle in your life starting today?

Part Five:

A Happier Life Through Greater Spiritual Well-Being

God's Plan of Happiness

The next four happiness principles we are going to discuss, all deal with ways of increasing our personal happiness through increasing the spiritual dimension of our lives. Before discussing these four principles, however, it might be beneficial for us to first take a look at a few underlying concepts about spirituality and God's plan of happiness for mankind, and how these relate to and can greatly enhance our own feelings of happiness.

The Three Degrees of Happiness

Just as there are three degrees of glory in the eternal worlds, I also believe that there are also three degrees of happiness in this life. Each is derived from a different source.

Telestial happiness is the temporary, fleeting gratification one receives from worldly pleasures. This kind of happiness is commonly associated with sin. As Latter-day Saints we know that we should stay clear of it, for ultimately it will lead us to sorrow and pain.

Many of the happiness principles that we have discussed thus far, such as improving our physical health and getting our finances under control, can be implemented without any understanding of God's plan of happiness. By applying correct principles a person can achieve some degree of happiness in this life without even believing that God exists. This is what we may call *terrestrial happiness*. This earthly (as opposed to worldly) happiness is good and is worthy of our pursuit.

In this regard, it is interesting to note that the Lord has taken the time to provide us with counsel and even some commandments on things that we might consider temporal or earthly in nature. For example, through His prophets the Lord has counseled us to "stay out of debt" and even explained to us how best to keep our bodies physically healthy (see D&C 89). These things are strictly of an earthly nature; after all, the inhabitants of the celestial kingdom don't have to worry about either balancing a checkbook or going on a diet. So, why does He give us counsel and laws governing such temporary, earthly things as finances and physical health? Because, as a loving Father, He wants us to maximize the happiness we are capable of experiencing—whether it be in this life or the next.

Life is tough enough without foolishly falling into pitfalls that we could easily avoid. God tells us how to avoid those pitfalls and also shows us the pathway that will lead us to the greatest possible happiness during our mortal experience. He shows us the way, and then, if we follow His counsel and choose wisely, we can experience terrestrial happiness.

Although it is very good, terrestrial happiness still falls far short of *celestial happiness*. This highest degree of happiness, as I mentioned in the preface of this book, is a feeling of "joy which none receiveth save it be the truly penitent and humble seeker of happiness" (that is, salvation; Alma 27:18). Celestial happiness comes to us directly from God. It is a fruit of the Spirit.

The Apostle Paul taught, "The fruit of the Spirit is love, joy, [and] peace" (Galatians 5:22). Love, joy, and peace are feelings or emotions that cause us to act with greater "gentleness, goodness, faith, meekness," and so forth (Galatians 5:22–23). In other words, these divine fruits or feelings, received through the Spirit, cause us to become more Christlike in our thoughts and actions. The celestial feelings of Godly peace and love, and the exhilarating joy that so often accompanies these divine emotions, is readily available to any "penitent and humble seeker of happiness" who actively seeks these fruits of the Spirit.

In a moment we will discuss how we can obtain these divine fruits, the ultimate feelings of happiness and joy. But first, let's take a brief look at some of the places such feelings of true celestial happiness will never be found.

Happiness Principle #11:

Avoid all pathways that promise happiness but lead to misery

Man is a happiness-seeking creature. Virtually everything he does, he does in an attempt to increase his feelings of happiness. Because of this, people don't consciously or intentionally set out to ruin their lives or make themselves miserable. But many end up doing just that by searching for happiness in all the wrong places.

We all have known and met individuals who mentally and physically appear to be mature adults, but who in their ability to make wise decisions and in terms of spiritual maturity are functioning at about the level of a two-year-old. They want immediate gratification for their appetites. They want their candy and they want it right now—even if it means foregoing far greater blessings, rewards, and happiness that they could receive in the near future if they could just learn to subdue and control their passions for a relatively brief moment in time.

Some hope to find happiness in a pub or bar, believing that alcohol, cigarettes, or drugs will take away their feelings of unhappiness and make them feel better. Others hope to find happiness from engaging in promiscuous sex, by trying to eat their troubles away, or by pursuing great wealth or power. While offering some temporary physical or emotional pleasure or gratification, none of these offer true happiness. In fact, just the opposite is usually true. Rather than offering real happiness, typically these things lead to disease, divorce, disability, depression, spiritual death, and, all too often, premature physical death. And what about the feelings of emptiness, low self-esteem, false pride, or guilt so often associated with these activities? Such practices are all quick fixes, all false roads that ultimately lead to unhappiness.

What the prophets of God have taught us is true: "wickedness never was happiness" (Alma 41:10). President Ezra Taft Benson said, "You cannot do wrong and feel right."[1]

Years ago when living in Cody, Wyoming, our family would regularly make the trip up to Billings, Montana, to attend the temple or to do some shopping. Along the highway between the two cities there are a number of markers planted in the soil just off the road. Each has been placed there by family members and friends of those who have been killed in highway accidents. At one particular location there are several crosses that mark the spot where four young college students crashed and died. Although these young men were not members of the Church, my eldest son Tad knew each of them fairly well, having played school basketball with several of them.

> Real happiness is cheap enough, yet how dearly we pay for its counterfeit.
> ~Hosea Ballou

Now to really understand teenagers, you need to understand the three "F's" that teens love the very best: freedom, fun, and friends. One particular night these four young men got together to enjoy their newfound freedom as college students doing what they thought would be great fun. However, instead of experiencing true happiness, after an evening of drunkenness and foolishness, they ended up as fatalities, the saddest of tragedies.

If used properly, the formula of freedom, fun, and friends can bring great felicity into a teenager's life. If used foolishly, as is all too often the case, it can be a formula for foolish fatalities.

These boys paid the ultimate price for their drinking and drunkenness. To be honest, I can think of absolutely nothing good that ever comes from this practice. During my own college years I recall having a friend describe to me the many experiences she had as a little girl cowering under her bed with fear when her father would come home drunk. She and her sister hid from him while her mother was verbally and physically abused by him. Imagine the mental and emotional abuse and scars she received from those childhood episodes. Years later, when I knew her, she was still receiving regular counseling sessions from university psychologists, trying to undo all of the emotional damage that had been done to her.

In speaking specifically of the negative effects of alcohol upon an individual, and on society as a whole, the First Presidency of the Church issued this statement in the October 1942 general conference:

> Drink brings cruelty into the home; it walks arm in arm with poverty; its companions are disease and plague; it puts chastity to flight; it knows neither honesty nor fair dealing; it is a total stranger to truth; it drowns conscience; it is the bodyguard of evil; it curses all who touch it.
>
> Drink has brought more woe and misery, broken more hearts, wrecked more homes, committed more crimes, filled more coffins, than all the wars the world has suffered.[2]

In our modern day and age, of course, much the same could be said of the plague of addictions coming from the use of illegal drugs, gambling, pornography, and sexual immorality.

If you would like to observe a group of people actively pursuing false happiness, visit a pub or bar. If you would like to see a group of people actively pursuing true happiness, you should visit a church. The Savior has made it clear that living the gospel is the only sure way to find true and lasting happiness. People may search and search, but they will never find it in any other way.

If You Are in a Bad Play, Go Write a New One!

If, after some real soul searching, you discover that you are on one of these dead end roads which promises happiness, but which you discover actually leads to unhappiness, then here is some wise advice for you:

If you don't like the scene you're in, if you are unhappy, if you're lonely, if you don't feel that things are happening, change your scene. Paint a new backdrop. Surround yourself with new actors. Write a new play—and if it's not a good play, get off the stage and write another one. There are millions of plays—as many as there are people. Leo Buscaglia.[3]

Yes, change your scene, write a new play, head down a new and better road—one that leads to true happiness. This may prove hard to do at first. If the old actors in your play don't want to be in this new play with you, you may have to find new actors for your play; new friends who will be there to guide and support you down this new road. It's your life, it's your happiness at stake. You are the lead actor in your own play; it's up to you to make your play a good one, a happy one.

Where True Happiness Can Be Found

Although happiness is the number one thing every person is seeking, it is interesting to note that when I was attending college there was not a university in the entire country that I am aware of that taught a class on this subject. Of course, this was not entirely true. Every religion class I attended at BYU, and every evening institute class I have attended since, have all taught me how to be happy. In each class I have been taught the principles of the gospel, and the whole purpose of the gospel of Jesus Christ is to show a person how to increase feelings of happiness in his or her life. Every sermon in sacrament meeting, every lesson taught in Sunday School has the same underlying goal in mind.

If you are truly serious about becoming happier, about making happiness your number one goal in life, you would be wise to attend church every Sunday, where you can be taught and regularly reminded of

> False happiness is like false money; it passes for a time as well as the true, and serves some ordinary occasions; but when it is brought to the touch, we find the lightness and alloy, and feel the loss.
> ~Alexander Pope

the principles of God's plan of happiness.

So, dear friend, identify and eliminate from your life any false substitutes for happiness (drugs, lust, greed, and so forth) that you may be currently pursuing. Attend church regularly. Stop looking for happiness in all the wrong places, and start looking for true happiness in all the right places.

Notes

1. Ezra Taft Benson, "Satan's Thrust—Youth," Ensign, Dec. 1971.
2. Conference Report, Oct. 1942, 8.
3. Meiji Stewart, *Happiness is an Inside Job* (Del Mar, California: Keep Coming Back Company, 1997), 92.

Happiness Principle #12:

Experience feelings of peace and joy through the Spirit

Worry is a happiness killer. There are a number of books, such as Dale Carnegie's *Stop Worrying and Start Living*, that provide some great tips on how to control this problem. If worrying is a problem in your life you may want to take a look at it. If you are losing sleep at night or having difficulties with high anxiety, the best solution is to find peace of mind through exercising faith in the Savior and by drawing the Comforter into your life.

Life was meant to be full of problems. Although it may seem odd and even contradictory, to experience some sadness and suffering in life is an integral and necessary part of God's plan of happiness. For you cannot fully enjoy and appreciate the sweet and happy times in life unless you have tasted and experienced some of the unpleasant and bitter ones. Our trials and difficulties help to perfect us and prepare us for a state of existence where we can one day experience a fullness of joy. As President Harold B. Lee explains:

> There is a refining process that comes through suffering, I think, that we can't experience any other way than by suffering. . . . We draw closer to Him who gave His life that man might be. We feel a kinship that we have never felt before. . . . He suffered more than we can ever imagine. But to the extent that we have suffered, somehow it seems to have the effect of

drawing us closer to the divine, helps to purify our souls, and helps to purge out the things that are not pleasing in the sight of the Lord.[1]

If life were continually just one big picnic or party for us, would we really need God? Would we need to humbly seek and plead for His help, His guidance, His spirit, or His love?

Although recognizing that trials and suffering are a necessary part of the refining process we must go through, such hardships and difficulties do not have to destroy our innermost feelings of peace. Yes, God has temporarily placed us in this refiner's fire, but in doing so He has also provided a way to greatly lessen and ease the suffering that typically accompanies the trials we each must face. For we can feel comfort and peace even in the most difficult of circumstances if we have drawn the Holy Ghost, or Comforter, to us.

> Happiness is the object and design of our existence; and will be the end thereof, if we pursue the path that leads to it; and this path is virtue, uprightness, faithfulness, holiness, and keeping all the commandments of God.
>
> ~Joseph Smith, Jr.

Earlier I mentioned celestial happiness is a fruit of the Spirit that a person can obtain only from God. Obviously, you can only enjoy the fruits of the Spirit if, indeed, you have the Spirit dwelling within you. The vital nature of having the Spirit in your life is clearly illustrated by an experience in the life of Brigham Young. Some months after the death of the Prophet Joseph Smith at Carthage Jail, he appeared to Brigham at Winter Quarters. During the course of their conversation, Brigham asked the Prophet what message Joseph would like him to give to the Saints. Joseph replied:

> Tell the people to get the Spirit of the Lord and it will lead them right. . . . They can tell the Spirit of the Lord from all other spirits; it will whisper *peace and joy* to their souls; it will take malice, hatred, strife and all evil from their hearts; and their whole desire will be to do good, bring forth righteousness

and build up the kingdom of God. Tell the brethren if they will follow the Spirit of the Lord, they will go right. Be sure to tell the people to keep the Spirit of the Lord.[2]

The Prophet Joseph could not have emphasized any more clearly the importance of having the Spirit in our lives, for without the Spirit it is impossible to experience the supreme feelings of peace, celestial happiness, and joy that we so greatly desire. Other blessings and gifts that we receive through the Spirit include the gift of faith, charity, personal revelation, priesthood power, and miracles, to name but a few. For all true happiness-seekers, one cannot help but see how vital it is to have the Spirit actively involved in one's life. So the question that naturally follows is: how do we draw the Spirit and His attendant blessings to us? There is no great mystery to this. As members of the Church we know that we bring the blessings of the Spirit into our lives by living the basic principles of the gospel of Jesus Christ as we have been taught to do.

The necessity of applying such basic principles as humility, faith, repentance, and prayer in one's life, and the resultant peace and joy that will follow by doing so, is clearly illustrated in the Book of Mormon. For example, near the end of his life, righteous King Benjamin gathered his people from all over the land so that he could teach them one last time before he passed on to the next life. After explaining the mission of Christ and His Atonement for their sins, the record states,

> [The people] had fallen to the earth, for the fear of the Lord had come upon them.
>
> And they had viewed themselves in their own carnal state, even less than the dust of the earth. And they all cried aloud with one voice, saying: O have mercy, and apply the atoning blood of Christ that we may receive forgiveness of our sins, and our hearts may be purified; for we believe in Jesus Christ, the Son of God, who created heaven and earth, and all things; who shall come down among the children of men.
>
> And it came to pass that after they had spoken these words

the *Spirit of the Lord* came upon them, and they were *filled with joy*, having received a remission of their sins, and having *peace of conscience*, because of their exceeding faith which they had in Jesus Christ who should come. (Mosiah 4:1-3; emphasis added)

As illustrated above, the Spirit, and the feelings of peace and joy are closely connected.

The importance of having the Spirit in my life, and of receiving the great blessing of peace that accompanies it, was strongly manifest to me during a fairly recent event in my life. My wife, Shelley, after observing several unusual spots on my skin, had made an appointment for me to see a doctor. This was done without my knowledge. It was something that I certainly never would have thought to do, since I considered them as common age spots. Upon informing me of what she had done, against my initial protests, she finally convinced me to keep the appointment. I considered this to be a complete waste of my time and money but decided to do it if it would make her happy. During the session several biopsies were taken. A week later the results of the tests came back: it was melanoma, the deadliest form of skin cancer. Had the cancer spread internally into other parts of my body? Into my vital organs? The doctor would not know until he began operating.

I learned of these test results on a Monday morning and my first operation to remove the cancerous growths was then scheduled to take place two days later.

During those two days I had some time to think deeply about my life up to that point in time, and what my life might be like in the months and years ahead. I was only fifty-five years old and, being the picture of health, had always anticipated living to be eighty years old or more. Was my life to be cut short twenty-five years? Was I prepared to go into the next life? Certainly I had lived a life far short of perfection. Nevertheless, I had lived worthy of attending the temple. I was eternally sealed to my wife and children. I had sought after and tried hard to live a life worthy of God's greatest blessings.

I must admit that during those two days of waiting, having prayed for the blessings of the Comforter in my life, I felt a great calmness. For whether I lived or died, it mattered not—the Lord's will be done concerning me. If I was soon to venture into the next life, I was prepared and eager to be a missionary for the Lord, taking the gospel to those spirits who had not had the opportunity to receive it during their life on earth. The only sadness and uneasiness I felt was from the thought of leaving my precious, sweet wife alone on earth for so many years to care for herself. I did not want her to suffer. Nevertheless, there was such a great feeling of peace knowing that she would forever be mine, and I would forever be hers. If we were to be separated, our time apart would only be for a brief moment when compared to the eternities that lay ahead. Together again, one day, we would enjoy an eternal family and all the riches of God's kingdom.

Well, fortunately this story has a happy ending (or obviously I wouldn't be here to tell it). The melanoma was caught early in its progression and surgically removed. My wife's inspiration to have me see a doctor, although against my wishes, ended up saving my life. She is so much farther along the pathway to perfection than I am; what would I do and be without her? How grateful I am to have her forever. How grateful I am for the divine Spirit that whispered peace to my soul in a time of trial and uncertainty.

> And moreover, I would desire that ye should consider on the blessed and happy state of those that keep the commandments of God. For behold, they are blessed in all things, both temporal and spiritual; and if they hold out faithful to the end they are received into heaven, that thereby they may dwell with God in a state of never-ending happiness. O remember, remember that these things are true; for the Lord God hath spoken it.
>
> ~King Benjamin
> (Mosiah 2:41)

In every prayer that we utter, we should ask our Heavenly Father for the blessing of the Spirit in our lives. This is critical. While in mortality we know that our lives will be filled with adversity; God has provided us with the gift of the Holy Ghost to bring us peace and hope during times of difficulty. Take full advantage of this blessing. Do not try to overcome life's trials by yourself. If you do as the Prophet Joseph said, you can have "the spirit whisper peace and joy" to your soul even during the most difficult times. Be wise and pray continually for the Spirit and His attendant blessings in your life.

Notes

1. Clyde J. Williams, ed., *The Teachings of Harold B. Lee*, (Salt Lake City, Utah: Bookcraft), 187–188.
2. Journal History of the Church, 23 Feb, 1847, as quoted in *Unlocking the Powers of Faith* by Garth L. Allred (American Fork, Utah: Covenant Communications, Inc., 1993), 44.

Happiness Principle #13:

Experience feelings of love and joy through the Spirit

All studies on happiness by social scientists indicate that religious people consistently rank higher on the happiness scale than those who are not religious. The only exception to this is among those individuals whose churches teach a false concept of God, believing that He is a very angry, vengeful, cruel, and demanding Being, rather than the perfectly loving, kind, just, and merciful Being that He really is. These studies further indicate that among those who consider themselves religious, regular church-goers consistently rank higher on the happiness scale than do those who don't attend church meetings.

Among members of the Lord's Church, it is obvious that the happiest Saints are those who are well along the pathway to being born again. The farther down this path they have traveled, the greater the feelings of celestial happiness they regularly experience.

From the teachings of the scriptures and our Church leaders, we know that to be born again involves more than just having a testimony of the truthfulness of the restored gospel. Although a testimony is required, becoming born again involves a gradual transformation or change that takes place in a person's life whereby they ultimately

> The supreme happiness of life is the conviction that we are loved.
>
> ~Victor Hugo

become a new creature in Christ (see 2 Corinthians 5:17). This change in a person's nature and character is brought about by the

Spirit, which the person has actively sought to bring into his life.

Such transformed individuals are totally devoted to Christ. Through the workings of the Spirit within them, they gradually come to think like Christ, and as a result, they gradually come to act like Christ. They are fully committed to building up His kingdom on earth. These Saints enjoy a peace of mind that "passeth all understanding" (Philippians 4:7). Through the Spirit, not only has the Savior removed their sins, but He has taken from them the very desire to sin. Rather than spend most of their time in prayer asking God to bless and to help them, they often spend much of their time in prayer asking God to reveal what they can do to help Him move forward His work.

As part of this transformation of spirit, there comes a feeling of charity, which is described in the scriptures as the "pure love of Christ" (Moroni 7:47). When you have gained this divine love in your heart, you will experience the ultimate feelings of happiness. This lesson is taught in the scriptures in the prophet Lehi's vision of the tree of life:

> And it came to pass that I beheld a tree, whose fruit was desirable to make one *happy*.
>
> And it came to pass that I did go forth and partake of the fruit thereof; and I beheld that it was most sweet, above all that I ever before tasted. Yea, and I beheld that the fruit thereof was white, to exceed all the whiteness that I had ever seen.
>
> And as I partook of the fruit thereof it filled my soul with *exceedingly great joy*; wherefore, I began to be desirous that my family should partake of it also; for I knew that it was *desirable above all other fruit*. (1 Nephi 8:10–12; emphasis added)

So what was this tree and fruit that Lehi had eaten that made him so remarkably happy? A few chapters later, Nephi is similarly shown this tree in vision, and learns the following:

> And I looked and beheld the virgin again, bearing a child in her arms.

> And the angel said unto me: Behold the Lamb of God, yea even the Son of the Eternal Father! Knowest thou the meaning of the tree which thy father saw?
>
> And I answered him, saying: Yea, it is the *love of God*, which sheddeth itself abroad in the hearts of the children of men; wherefore, it is the *most desirable above all things*.
>
> And he spake unto me, saying: Yea, and the *most joyous* to the soul. (1 Nephi 11:20–23; emphasis added)

From these verses it becomes apparent that the pure love of God (which is the "most desirable above all things") and true happiness (joy) are inseparably tied together. The one (pure love) automatically leads to the other (pure joy). This truth is illustrated once again in the scriptures by Mormon's description of the converted Nephites and Lamanites who lived in America shortly after the Savior's visit there:

> And it came to pass that there was no contention in the land, because of the *love of God* which did dwell in the hearts of the people.
>
> And there were no envyings, nor strifes, nor tumults, nor whoredoms, nor lyings, nor murders, nor any manner of lasciviousness; and surely there could not be a *happier people* among all the people who had been created by the hand of God. (4 Nephi 1:15–16; emphasis added)

According to Mormon, there could not be a happier people on the face of the earth than were these people. What made them so happy? It was a result of the pure love of God that had come into their hearts. Because of this love, they had lost all desire to sin or live wickedly.

How would you like to feel the love, peace, and happiness that these people felt? It is possible to do, but it does take some work to achieve.

Feelings of charity and the celestial happiness that always

accompanies such Christlike love do not come into our hearts automatically or without effort on our part. To receive these fruits of the Spirit, not only must we keep our thoughts pure and our actions righteous, but we must also ask God for these fruits or feelings through fervent, humble prayer. As the prophet Mormon taught:

> But charity is the pure love of Christ, and it endureth forever; and whoso is found possessed of it at the last day, it shall be well with him.

> Wherefore, my beloved brethren, *pray unto the Father with all the energy of heart, that ye may be filled with this love*. (Moroni 7:47–48; emphasis added)

God wants us to clearly recognize the source of this gift of love in our lives, so He requires us to ask for it. We must be "penitent and humble" seekers of love and happiness (Alma 27:18). That is, we must come before God with a broken heart and contrite spirit, humbly pleading for His forgiveness for our sins, requesting His Spirit to be with us, and asking to feel of His divine love for us. As we come to feel of His love for us, in turn we will feel our love increasing and flowing back to Him. Ultimately His love will fill our hearts, flowing through us and out toward all those around us.

> Life is fortified by many friendships. To love, and to be loved, is the greatest happiness of existence.
> ~Sydney Smith

The pure love of Christ, and the joy that is associated with it, is "the most desirable" thing that we can ever seek in this life. To obtain it is worth any sacrifice.

To achieve the greatest feelings of love, peace, and happiness in this life and the next, we must look to the Savior. We must pray with all the energy of our hearts for these sweet fruits of the Spirit. Only He can take our sins and guilt from us. Only He can fill our hearts with celestial love and joy. Ultimately, our greatest feelings of happiness will come through Him.

Happiness Principle #14:

Be actively involved in a good cause

An essential element of a happy life is the need to experience the joy associated with selfless service. As we seek and ultimately receive the pure love of Christ in our hearts, there comes a longing within us to share that love with others. During the process of becoming born again, we begin to move beyond doing good works simply out of a sense of duty. We begin doing good because we are good. We start to become like Christ.

As part of His plan of happiness the Lord has counseled that "men should be anxiously engaged in a good cause, and do many things of their own free will, and bring to pass much righteousness" (D&C 58:27). Happy is the person who is actively involved in a good cause.

There is a need within each of us to feel fulfilled, to feel like our life has meaning, that we can make a difference, and that the world is a better place for us having lived here. We all need a worthy cause to lose ourselves in. As author George Bernard Shaw once stated: "This is the true joy of life, being used up for a purpose recognized by yourself as a mighty one."[1]

Unfortunately, far too many people miss out on this opportunity to feel the joy and fulfillment associated with doing good, choosing instead to focus inwardly, to live selfishly, and to do little more than exist. They fall into a routine of getting up in the morning, eating, going to work, coming home from work, eating, watching TV, and going to bed. This schedule is repeated over and over again, only broken by a weekend activity of seeking some worldly pleasure to satisfy themselves.

There is no real joy in a life that never experiences the blessings of loving and lifting others.

What Is Your Personal Mission in Life?

Most people who describe themselves as truly happy have sought for and found their special mission or personal calling in life. This calling becomes the central focus of their lives, directing their energy toward the passionate pursuit and advancement of a special cause. Such a calling provides deep purpose and meaning for one's life. In his insightful book, *The Joy of Not Working*, author Ernie Zelinski states:

> One of the chief sources of happiness is having a special purpose or personal mission in life.
>
> Your personal mission has nothing to do with making money. Having a personal mission or purpose means utilizing your unique talents in such a way that enhances conditions for humanity. Your life is also enhanced because of the satisfaction and happiness you experience.[2]

Zelinski goes on to note that for some individuals their personal mission might be to reduce pollution or to improve the environment. It may be to create wonderful works of music or art to be enjoyed by mankind. It may be something as simple as teaching children how to excel at playing basketball or the piano. For some, it may be found in preparing young men for life by helping them to become Eagle Scouts. All of these activities are of benefit to mankind and, if your interest in it is great enough, they can be pursued with passion.

> Service to a just cause rewards the worker with more real happiness and satisfaction than any other venture in life.
>
> ~Carrie Chapman Catt

If you are gifted on the piano, using this talent to teach children to also play the piano is a wonderful personal mission. But for a

Latter-day Saint, this would obviously be a secondary calling. As noted in the preface, your overarching or primary personal mission is the same as mine and that of all Church members: to live worthy to return to God one day and to take your family and as many other people as possible along with you.

Consider for a moment all the many great causes on earth that a person could possibly be engaged in. Now, of all these wonderful causes or missions, which one would God consider the greatest? It would be, of course, to be actively engaged in His "work and [His] glory, to bring to pass the immortality and eternal life of man" (Moses 1:39). As such, our personal mission is similar to the three-fold mission of the Church: 1) to perform missionary work, 2) to redeem the dead, and 3) to perfect the Saints. All three of these are focused on the salvation of mankind, our primary personal mission in life.

> I don't know what your destiny will be, but one thing I know: the only ones among you who will be truly happy are those who have sought and found a way to serve.
>
> ~Albert Schweitzer

As members of the Lord's Church, we are fortunate to have opportunities readily available to us to serve others. From this service flows joy. Every position we hold and perform in the Church is tied to this three-fold mission, whether it be teaching a Primary class, holding a leadership position, doing genealogy work, attending the temple, reactivating and doing missionary work, or serving as a home or visiting teacher. Every calling we perform and every assignment we fulfill, is an opportunity for us to move God's work forward and to bless the lives of others. We are actively engaged in the greatest cause on earth. What could possibly bring us greater feelings of happiness and fulfillment than this?

Of course, service to others is not limited to our work in the Church. There are many other good causes a person can choose to become actively involved in. These might include caring for a sick or elderly spouse or parent, shoveling snow from a neighbor's sidewalk, serving on the local school board or PTA, or volunteering at a local food bank or homeless shelter. The list is endless. Whether our service is directed toward just one individual or toward an entire community or nation, the result is the same—an increase in the happy feelings in our hearts.

At the end of each day our feelings of success should not come from examining how much money we earned or how much fun we had. But rather they should come from considering such questions as, "How many lives did I touch for good? How many souls did I lift? How many sincere compliments did I utter? How much encouragement did I provide?" A good question to ask ourselves at the end of each day might be, "Today, was I perhaps the answer to somebody's prayer?"

Never Retire from Serving

We all tend to dream of the day when we can retire, when we can just lay around doing little or nothing, as we please. The truth is, however, that work, not leisure, actually brings us more happiness. For example, studies done of lottery winners show that after six months of spending their winnings on travel and leisure these people find themselves being no more happy than they were prior to hitting the jackpot. Nearly all of them go back to work. They discover that they need a reason for getting out of bed each morning. They want to feel like they have accomplished something worthwhile during the day, that their lives have meaning, and that they have done some good in the world.

> Half the world is on the wrong scent in the pursuit of happiness. . . . They think it consists in having and getting. . . . On the contrary, it consists in giving, and in serving.
> ~Henry Drummond

I have an uncle who spent his entire professional career as a professor at BYU. At retirement time he didn't retire, he just changed employers, going to work full-time for the Lord. He and my aunt sold their house and most of their personal belongings. They have spent about the last ten years of their lives serving various types of missions for the Church. In between missions they travel the country visiting their children, grandchildren, and friends. Not only are they staying active and busy working, but they are working in the greatest cause on earth. It's a perfect formula for feeling love and joy. I've never known a happier couple. Shelley and I plan to follow their example. At retirement we plan to stay active doing humanitarian, temple, and missionary work. What about you?

Increase the happiness in your life by finding ways to be of greater service to others. Lose yourself in service to God.

Notes

1. Meiji Stewart, *Happiness is an Inside Job* (Del Mar, California: Keep Coming Back Company, 1997), 66.
2. Ernie J. Zelinski, *The Joy of Not Working* (Berkeley, California: Ten Speed Press, 2003), 57, 60.

Part Six:

A Happier Life
Through Greater
Emotional Well-Being

Happiness Principle #15:

Live in the present

People who spend too much time thinking about mistakes or lost opportunities in the past are usually unhappy or even depressed. Although recalling fond memories from the past can be wonderful and temporarily make us feel happy, even these, if dwelt upon too often or too deeply, can make us unhappy with our present situation, if we constantly long for the good old days.

Similarly, spending too much time thinking about the future can create unhappiness in our lives. We can make ourselves both emotionally and physically sick by thinking about something terrible that might happen tomorrow or next week to us or to someone we love. Or we may find ourselves feeling that we just can't be happy until some future event takes place or some goal is met.

This is not to say that having something to look forward to is bad. It is quite the opposite. Knowing that we have a date or another activity to attend on the weekend with our spouse or friend can certainly make an otherwise routine or uneventful week more bearable. Anticipating an event can be almost as enjoyable as attending the event itself. But even so, as a general rule, happy people spend relatively little time thinking about either the past or the future. They live their lives in the present, fully experiencing and enjoying each event of the day as it unfolds.

When a happy person talks to another person he or she is attentive, listening closely and trying to understand what the other person is thinking and feeling. Unhappy people, on the other hand, often find their minds wandering during a conversation, as they focus on some past or future event rather than on the present.

Enjoy Each Chapter of Your Life

The nineteenth century English clergyman, essayist, and wit, Sydney Smith once wrote, "The haunts of happiness are varied, but I have more often found her among little children, home firesides, and country houses than anywhere else."[1]

This is a perfect description of the life Shelley and I led when our children were young. Our family lived in a country farmhouse, our closest neighbors living about a half mile away. With no neighborhood children to play with, our children played with each other and we all became best friends. So many fond memories. Those were truly some happy days for me.

Time has passed since then. We have moved to town. Our four oldest children have left home—gone to college, gone to the mission field, and gone to the temple to be married. In just a few more years our two youngest will also depart, leaving Shelley and I to cope with an empty nest. We deeply love each of our children and miss them so much when they are away from us. We look forward to those brief times when they can be with us. And yet, the truth is

> If you wish to be happy, we'll tell you the way: don't live tomorrow till you've lived today.
>
> ~Author Unknown

that even though this great source of joy is physically moving away from us, we continue to stay busy and to live happily in our present circumstances, discovering new sources of joy each day.

We all experience many different chapters in our lives, and each can be filled with activity, with love, and with joy if we so choose. The American Quaker theologian Elton Trueblood understood this truth when he wrote: "I keep thinking of the wisdom of Aristotle when he affirmed that happiness cannot be achieved in less than a complete lifetime. This means that the last chapter is just as important as any other. It is good to be young and it is good to be old. Life is lived best if it is lived in chapters and knowing which chapter one is in and not to pine for what is not."[2]

So, if you want to increase your feelings of happiness, stay focused on the present. Enjoy today! Relish the moment! Live your life in chapters, and in this chapter, truly experience and find joy in each event that life affords you!

Notes

1. www.madwed.com/quotes/Quotations/Stories/Habits_Happiness/ body_habits_happiness.html.
2. www.lectionaid.com/Sample/LA040702.

Happiness Principle #16:

Increase your self-esteem

People possessing high self-esteem are people that feel good about themselves. Obviously, they are much happier than people with low self-esteem who do not feel good about themselves. Since feelings of self-esteem and feelings of happiness are so closely associated, it is important to understand how we can increase our feelings of self-worth, or self-esteem, so that we can similarly increase our feelings of happiness.

When people are young most of their feelings of self-worth come from outside of themselves. How they are treated by their parents and schoolmates, how they perceive their own physical appearance, and how much recognition they receive for their personal achievements all greatly affect their self-esteem. If they are teased or belittled by peers or parents, their self-esteem goes down. If they are the class president, the captain of the football team, or the homecoming queen, they feel popular and their self-esteem goes up.

When a person achieves a goal of his choosing, the result is positive and results in an increase of what we might call terrestrial self-esteem. When he achieves a goal of someone else's choosing to please or impress others, it is of much less value in building self-esteem or increasing happiness. If achieving a goal creates feelings of superiority, pride, or vanity, it is simply creating telestial self-esteem and is detrimental to his spiritual growth.

As we grow older and wiser we learn that self-esteem gained from external sources is only temporary in nature. In college you soon learn that nobody cares if you were once a high school basketball star or captain of the drill team. The glory you once received, and the self-esteem you gained from it, has become a thing of the past. Similarly, over time, the physical beauty that the homecoming queen possesses will diminish, eventually being replaced with wrinkled skin and gray hair. Self-esteem that is tied closely to the honors and applause of men, or to one's good looks, is destined to eventually fade away.

Even as adults we appreciate an occasional pat on the back or an honest compliment. And we do feel more confident when we look our best. We enjoy a little stroke of our egos by others every now and then. However, if this external source becomes our sole source of self-esteem, that is, if we must continually have validation from others in order to feel worthwhile, then we will find ourselves living on an emotional roller coaster. As author M. J. Ryan notes:

> It's as if we've given the key to the safety deposit box that holds our life savings [our self-esteem] to someone else. We can't access it ourselves; we have to go through them. What if they leave? What if they die, and we can't find the key? What if they steal the box? We can never experience true inner peace and contentment, because we're always wondering if the person with the key is going to disappear.[1]

When you give to others control over your self-esteem, you simultaneously surrender to them control over your feelings of happiness or unhappiness.

Rather than spend one's entire life seeking acceptance from external sources, by constantly trying to impress or please others, a much stronger and more consistent source of self-worth can come from internal sources, by pleasing ourselves and God. This true and lasting celestial self-esteem springs up within us in two ways. First, it comes into our minds as we begin to understand who we really are. It comes as we recognize that we are something far greater than a sports star or a beauty queen. We are sons and daughters of God! We are of royal birth, princes or princesses, destined to sit on thrones as kings and queens. I don't mean this in a fairy tale sense. We really are destined to rule over kingdoms.

The second way to increase true and lasting self-esteem in our hearts, is to change our hearts for the better. It comes to us as we begin to live like the persons of divine, royal lineage that we are. We feel good about ourselves when we know that we are living right, and that our actions are in line with our inner values. We feel a harmony within us that creates a peaceful, confident feeling. As the Mohandas

> Love yourself, for if you don't, how can you expect anybody else to love you?
> ~Author unknown

K. Gandhi, once stated, "Happiness is when what you think, what you say, and what you do are in harmony."[2]

Although the physical beauty of our once youthful bodies will diminish as we grow older, the beauty of our spirits can be, and should be, constantly growing greater. As it does, our self-esteem and feelings of happiness will also greatly increase.

Unhappy people with a low self-image often criticize, gossip about, and find fault in others. They are jealous of the success of others and seek reasons to tear down and to criticize rather than to build up. They rejoice over the misfortunes and failures of those they secretly envy. On the other hand, happy people with high self-esteem are quick to lift, compliment, and encourage others. They find no joy in others' problems, weaknesses, or failures. Their self-image is not threatened or affected by the success of others. They are happy when others succeed and are always among the first to genuinely and enthusiastically congratulate them.

Two Self-esteem and Happiness Killers

Now, there are two happiness killers commonly associated with self-esteem of which Latter-day Saints should be particularly wary. Both were illustrated in a documentary titled *Mormon Women and Depression*, which aired on television a number of years ago (1979, directed by Louise Degn).

In this documentary several LDS women were interviewed. Each of these sisters suffered from low self-esteem and depression. As they spoke, it became apparent that one reason they had become depressed was that they regularly compared their performance in the gospel to that of other LDS women. When they did so, nearly without exception, they found themselves coming up short. Other women always seemed to have a cleaner house and better behaved children and were spiritually far superior to them. Other women seemed to be super moms and super homemakers while the women interviewed felt like super duds. Such comparisons made them feel inferior and ultimately led them to a deep sadness.

The second cause of low self-esteem and depression among these women was that they felt overwhelmed by what was required of them. In order to reap salvation they felt they needed to be perfect in every way. They needed to be the perfect mom, the perfect homemaker, the perfect wife, the perfect church member, and perfect in living the gospel in every way. With checklist in hand, they had thought that by a zealous, nearly fanatical performance of good works they could be their own saviors. But for some reason, it just wasn't working. Greatly discouraged, and having lost the Spirit, they were certain they could never qualify for the celestial kingdom, no matter how hard they tried.

> Why compare yourself to others? No one in the entire world can do a better job of being you than you.
> ~Author unknown

These women failed to understand that the Church and gospel were not instituted by the Lord to make us miserable. They were created to make us happy. The gospel of Jesus Christ is not bad news, it is the good news.

These sisters had made the mistake of comparing themselves to others or to a standard of perfection that would be virtually impossible to attain in this life. They failed to understand two things. First, we should never compare our performance to that of others. If we do, we will determine ourselves to be either above or beneath them. This will lead to feelings of self-righteousness and pride on the one hand, or to feelings of inferiority and envy on the other, both of which are telestial self-esteem. In either case we will become less Christlike and lose our inner harmony. As a result, our true self-esteem and happiness will be diminished.

Second, these sisters failed to understand that the Lord doesn't expect a person to "run faster than he has strength" (Mosiah 4:27). As Elder Bruce R. McConkie once stated, you don't have to be "truer than true" in living the gospel to attain salvation. You just have to stay in the "mainstream of the Church," doing those things that good, down-to-earth Latter-day Saints do.[3] As long as you are headed in the right direction and pressing forward, ultimately you will end up exactly where you want to be: experiencing a fullness of joy while living with God, His Son, and with all those that you love the most.

Live the gospel, love the gospel, but don't become fanatical about the gospel. Lighten up, enjoy the trip, and realize that you are doing okay. Just stay on the right path and head in the right direction. If you do, you will feel good about yourself and happiness will be your eternal traveling companion.

Notes

1. M. J. Ryan, *365 Health and Happiness Boosters* (York Beach, Maine: Conari Press, 2000), 176.

2. www.widomquotes.com/cat_happiness.html.

3. Bruce R. McConkie, "The Effects Flowing from the Divine Sonship," *Sermons and Writings of Bruce R. McConkie* (Salt Lake City, Utah: Bookcraft, 1989), 66.

Happiness Principle #17:

Eliminate guilt and grudges

Happiness is a good feeling or emotion that we feel inside us. As with any other emotion that we feel, happiness is created and directly affected by what we are thinking. If we are thinking good, positive thoughts we will experience good, positive emotions. If we are thinking bad, negative thoughts we will experience bad, negative emotions.

Psychologists tell us that when a person's mind is not actively involved in organized thinking, his thoughts will naturally drift toward a state of chaos. In other words, when not consciously directed, a person's mind will begin to wander, producing thoughts on all sorts of topics one right after another. In such a mental state, eventually thoughts about problems or concerns will begin to surface. If a person then begins to focus his attention on these negative thoughts, eventually these ideas will begin to create negative emotions such as worry, stress, fear, anger, depression, guilt, regret, resentment, and so forth. Happiness and peace of mind cannot dwell within us at the same time we are experiencing such negative emotions.

So how do we go about ridding ourselves of negative thoughts and emotions we don't like, so that we can make room for the more positive thoughts and emotions that we do like? The most effective method is to get to the root of a particular problem that is causing the bad feelings, and get rid of it. In other words, solve the problem and forget it. To illustrate how we might do this, let's take as examples two negative emotions, guilt and resentment, and see how we can rid ourselves of them.

Get Rid of Guilt

When we start thinking about our lives and the things we have done that are wrong, we begin to feel guilty. This is a natural, inborn response to sin. Guilt is an emotion brought about by our conscience, a manifestation of the light of Christ with which we were born.

Obviously, the more we can bring our actions into conformity with our gospel beliefs and values, the less we will be sinning and thus the less we will feel guilt. That is the ultimate solution—just don't sin. Realizing, however, that none of us are perfect yet, and that we all have sinned and will likely yet sin, how do we eliminate the guilt we feel? The answer is quite simple. We get rid of guilt by looking to the Savior. Through proper repentance, the Savior can take our sins and guilt from us.

A number of years ago while serving as a bishop, I had an elderly sister come to my office. She had come to confess a sin. While in her early twenties, prior to being active in the Church, she had become pregnant out of wedlock and had solved her dilemma by having an abortion. Not long after this she became active in the Church and had been a faithful member ever since. Because of her many years of faithfulness, her confession to me was not the beginning of the repentance process but rather the culmination of it. She left my office that day knowing of the Savior's love for her, at last having lifted from her shoulders the heavy burden of deep guilt she had experienced for some fifty years. What a tragedy that she had allowed herself to suffer this negative, happiness-destroying feeling for so many years.

> We cannot change the past, but we can change our attitude toward it. Uproot guilt and plant forgiveness. Tear out arrogance and seed humility. Exchange love for hate—thereby, making the present comfortable and the future promising.
> ~Maya Angelou

Any sin that goes unrepented of is a potential happiness killer. This is particularly true of the more serious sins such as those dealing with sexual immorality. If you have had a problem in this area, go in and talk to your bishop as soon as you can. The Lord has ordained him as a judge in Israel, not to condemn you but to love, help, and lift you. Yes, it will be difficult and will take some courage to go in and see him. You may experience some degree of self-inflicted humiliation or embarrassment in doing so. Like it or not, the Lord has made this part of the repentance process. Keep in mind, however, that it is far easier to feel a little discomfort now than to choose the alternative. Just try to imagine the guilt, shame, and sorrow you will feel one day if required to stand before the Savior in an unclean and unrepentant state.

Yes, the repentance process does begin with feeling guilt, sorrow, sadness and a multitude of other negative emotions. The good news, however, is that once you have repented you end up feeling the wonderful, positive emotions of peace, love, and joy. The bishop is there to help bring you back to this happy state of mind. If you need to repent, don't procrastinate. Get it done. To wait is only to prolong your suffering, when you could be feeling clean, worthy, and happy once again.

Get Rid of Grudges

For many, one of the most difficult commandments that the Savior gave to mankind was the requirement to forgive all those whom we feel have wronged us. Although often very difficult to do, as we really think about it, we come to realize that the Lord actually gave us this commandment to help us be happier. If we aren't able to forgive others, think of the damage that we do to ourselves. For example, think of the many thousands of people worldwide who have gone inactive in the Church because of some unkind word spoken toward them by another Church member. Who are these people hurting by staying away from church? Only themselves, of course. On top of this, think of the unhappiness we bring upon ourselves by harboring such negative thoughts and feelings.

Anger, resentment, and hatred toward others who may have offended us are all destructive, negative feelings that prevent us from enjoying the feelings of peace, love, and joy that we want to have.

On a number of occasions while serving as a bishop, I had

middle-aged women come in to visit with me concerning the abuse they had suffered as children. Some of these sisters had suffered physical or sexual abuse, and all had suffered emotional abuse. In an attempt to relieve themselves of the anger, guilt, hatred, or other negative emotions they felt, many had been receiving regular therapy from professional counselors and psychiatrists. They wanted to be able to forgive and forget with all their heart because they knew that until they did, they would never feel the peace inside they so desperately desired. Nevertheless, it seemed that no matter how hard they tried, no matter how much counseling or good advice they received, their hurt was so deep that they simply could not forgive the person who had abused them.

Once again, the solution to the problem lies with the Savior. Some problems are just too large for us to solve on our own. Christ has promised to lift our burdens from us if we will ask Him to. He is the Prince of Peace. He can bring peace to our minds, removing from us anger, resentment, and hatred, when we are unable to do it ourselves. If you are suffering from such feelings, I would suggest that you plead with Him to lift these feelings from you. And if you are penitent, persistent, fervent, and humble in your prayers to God, He will remove the pain from you, soothe your soul, and fill your heart with peace.

Turn to the Lord to rid yourself of guilt and grudges. Replace all the bad feelings you are experiencing in your life with good feelings of peace, love, and joy. Take full advantage of the many blessings that are part of God's plan of happiness for you.

Happiness Principle #18:

Develop a good sense of humor and an optimistic, enthusiastic attitude

Laughter reduces emotional stress and can actually have a positive effect on your physical body as well. There are documented stories of people being healed from life-threatening diseases by watching funny movies on a daily basis. A recent medical study indicated that a regular dose of laughter can reduce the risk of a heart attack by as much as 50 percent. People possessing a good sense of humor, who laugh frequently and freely, typically live much longer and healthier lives than do sourpusses.

The Lord regularly counseled His disciples to "be of good cheer" (Matthew 9:2, 14:27; John 16:33; Acts 23:11). The Prophet Joseph Smith described himself as having a "cheery temperament" (Joseph Smith—History 1:28). And those familiar with some of our modern-day prophets, such as Gordon B. Hinckley and Thomas S. Monson, know what wonderful senses of humor they have. So lighten up, learn a few good jokes, be quick to smile, and brighten up your own life as well as the lives of others.

Attitude Is Everything

It doesn't take a scientific study for one to realize that a person with an optimistic, enthusiastic, and positive attitude about life is going to be a lot happier than a perpetual grouch. How is your attitude? Do you ever wake up in the morning feeling grumpy, expecting little more than to have to drag yourself through another pathetic day? Are you the type who believes that happiness may be just around the next corner in life, but is never here to experience right now? Well, if this is the way you feel, then maybe it's time to give yourself an attitude adjustment. It's time to use your God-given freedom to start choosing to be positive and happy instead of negative and grumpy. Here's a suggestion on how you might begin.

One of the best ways to start down the path to a happy day is to decide to be happy and then to begin acting like you really are, right away. Remember, your thoughts control your feelings, so in reality you are only one pleasant thought away from a good, happy feeling. In essence, you psych yourself up into feeling happy. You may think this is just being phony, and initially it may feel that way, but after awhile you will find that it won't be an act anymore. You will actually start to feel better.

Wake up early in the morning so that you have sufficient time to read the scriptures, pray, and meditate. This will provide you with an underlying calm, peaceful feeling to start your day. Then spend at least twenty minutes doing aerobic exercise. That'll wake you up, get your blood flowing, and energize you. In the shower and while driving to work, sing a hymn, such as "Scatter Sunshine," "There Is Sunshine in My Soul Today," and "Count Your Blessings." Sing with enthusiasm—use your best opera voice and turn up the volume!

When you sit or stand, keep your back straight, your head up, and your shoulders back. When you walk, look ahead, swing your arms, and take long strides. Studies show that these techniques actually increase your feelings of happiness, whereas slouching or shuffling along taking short steps with eyes cast downward have the opposite effect. As you greet people, smile. Again, studies show that there is something that actually happens to a person psychologically just by turning up the corners of his or her mouth. But it needs to be a BIG smile, one that raises the cheeks. In his book *The Pursuit of Happiness*, Dr.

> I realize that a sense of humor isn't for everyone. It's only for people who want to have fun, enjoy life, and feel alive.
> ~Anne Wilson Schaef

David Myers notes:

> Surely you've noticed. You're in a testy mood. But when the phone rings, you feign cheer while talking to your friend. Strangely, after hanging up, you no longer feel so grumpy. Such is the value of social occasions—calls, visits, dinners out: They impel us to behave as if we were happy, which in fact helps free us from our unhappiness.[1]

Granted, these techniques do not always work; particularly if you are in the midst of a terribly trying ordeal in your life. But under normal circumstances they almost always do. So give it a try. Start by simply singing or whistling a happy tune, sitting or standing up straight, swinging your arms while taking a brisk walk, smiling broadly while passing or when greeting others, and socializing and laughing with a

> All you need in the world is love and laughter. That's all anybody needs. To have love in one hand and laughter in the other.
>
> ~August Wilson

friend. Lighten up, learn a few good jokes, be quick to smile, and brighten up your own life as well as the lives of others. Then sit back and enjoy the good, happy feelings that begin to emerge. It's not so difficult. You can do it!

Notes

1. David Myers, *The Pursuit of Happiness* (New York: William Morrow and Company, Inc., 1992), 125.

Set Goals and Apply the Principles

Magazine publisher Malcolm Forbes stated: "When what we are is what we want to be, that's happiness."[1]

With this truth in mind, may I be so bold as to ask, what are you? Or more specifically, what are you physically: healthy or unhealthy? What are you financially: secure or heavily in debt? What are you socially: married happily or unhappily? What are you spiritually? Mentally? Emotionally?

Now let me ask, what do you want to be? Think about it. Do you want to be happily married? Guilt-free? Healthy and energetic? Free from debt? Well-educated? Perhaps a professional or self-employed individual? A full-time homemaker? Someone with high self-esteem? Filled with love and joy? If you could, what would you be?

Finally, permit me to ask, what would you have to do in order to become what you want to be?

A good place to start would be to begin applying in your life the eighteen happiness principles that we have discussed. Rather than drifting through life, dreaming about someday being happier and more successful, get off the couch, take control of your life, and get serious about improving the quality of your life experience.

As you have read this book, I hope you have chosen some goals that will help increase feelings of happiness in your life. Perhaps you have set goals to improve your physical health, get out of debt, and draw the Spirit of the Lord more fully into your life. A word of caution about choosing these, and other secondary happiness goals. In reality,

> The foolish man seeks happiness in the distance; the wise grows it under his feet.
> ~James Oppenheim

getting into better physical shape and getting out of debt may take you months to accomplish. Drawing the Spirit ever more closely to you is a lifetime task. Do not wait until these goals are fully accomplished to enjoy a feeling of happiness. Instead, you can choose to be happy right now.

Choose to Be Happy Right Now

The 1993 Price Entertainment movie "Shadowlands" depicts a portion of the life of popular English author and philosopher, C. S. Lewis. In this film, Lewis describes a group of people who "live in the shadowlands . . . [where] the sun is always shining somewhere else—around the bend in the road, over the brow of the hills." For these folks happiness is always just barely out of reach . . . never to be enjoyed here and now.[2]

So often people feel that they just can't be happy until some particular goal is accomplished or future event occurs in their life. For example, some will say, "I just can't be happy until I am married," "I just can't be happy until I have children, or, "I just can't be happy until I graduate from college and start my career." Then, once they finally achieve their goal, they are happy for only a moment before they complain, "I just can't be happy until . . ." It's difficult to find happiness if you live in Shadowland.

> Happiness is not a state you arrive at, but a manner of traveling.
> ~Margaret Lee Runbeck

Happy people most certainly have goals. But the point is, they don't wait until their goals are fully accomplished to reward themselves with a feeling of happiness. They experience happiness each day of their lives as they work toward their goals. They know that happiness can be felt all along the journey, not just upon their arrival at the destination.

The same can be true with each of us. We need not tie our happiness to our accomplishments. For what if we never achieve all of our goals in life? Are we then to never experience or enjoy happiness?

If happiness is what we truly desire, then why live in shadowlands and put hills or mountains in our way? A wise man, who has made the achievement of happiness his number one goal in life, once stated: "No reason to make happiness the dessert on the menu; it can be the whole meal."[3]

When God placed us upon the earth, He allowed us freedom of choice. Besides being free to choose between good and evil, righteousness and wickedness, we are also free to choose our attitudes whether they be positive or negative. We can choose faith over doubt, love over hate, and even happiness over sadness. God put us in control of our thoughts, and the thoughts we freely choose to embrace control our attitudes, our feelings, and ultimately our actions.

People who describe themselves as being very happy or extremely happy have made the choice to feel happy feelings right now. So, if you want to be really happy, don't put it off until tomorrow, choose to be happy today.

Notes

1. www.entplaza.com
2. "The Pageant of Learning," *Shadowlands*, DVD, directed by Richard Attenborough (1994; New York, NY: HBO Home Video, 1999).
3. Barry Neil Kaufman, *Happiness is a Choice* (New York, New York: Ballantine Books, 1994), 183.

The Effect of Earthly Tests and Trials On Our Pursuit of Happiness

I hope that I haven't left you with a false impression that a person can feel great continual happiness each and every minute and hour of his life, or that happiness is easily captured. I do not want to appear like a naïve Pollyanna. I know only too well that we have come from a celestial home on high and are now temporarily dwelling in a telestial world. It is a little like being a fish out of water—we are out of our natural element. While dwelling in this fallen world, we will never attain the full and constant feelings of celestial happiness that we will enjoy in the life to come. Life in mortality will never be perfect for us.

Besides the little annoyances that daily crop up, the truth is, there will also be times in each of our lives when happiness seems to flee from us for awhile as we undergo a major trial. This is to be expected. The plan has always been that we will learn patience, humility, faith, and other godly attributes by traveling through the refiner's fire of mortality. Your major trial may come in the form of a difficult personal relationship, poor health, a financial setback, or any one of a score of other problems.

Certainly, if we want to maximize our happiness, we should try to do all we can to minimize the number and effect of these trials in our lives. To do this we need to be aware that there are two basic kinds of trials we experience here on earth. First, there are those trials that come upon us naturally, that we can do little or nothing to prevent; and second, there are those that are self-inflicted, those that we bring upon ourselves because of our own poor decisions. Although there are certain trials we each must go through from which we can grow and benefit, certainly there are many others that are of little or no benefit to us and only bring us unneeded misery. Life is difficult enough without our adding to our problems and difficulties.

Regarding these self-inflicted trials that come upon us from making poor decisions, consider, for example, what results when a young person decides to drop out of high school before graduating. He is almost guaranteed a life of poverty, or near poverty, living on little more than a minimum wage income. As we learned earlier, poverty and unhappiness largely go hand-in-hand. If you want to live a happy life, is dropping out of school early a wise decision to make? Hardly. A person who does so is simply choosing extra, unneeded misery in his life that is of absolutely no benefit to him.

I know a man who, when he was young, was very personable, good looking, intelligent, and well-liked. He was the type of individual that you could see was destined to go far in life. However, in his teenage years he made a foolish decision and became hooked on drugs—a problem he has struggled with his entire adult life. Largely as a result of this addiction he has been divorced twice and has spent time in jail and in the state penitentiary. His drug use has caused brain cell damage and as a result he has learning and memory disabilities and has had great difficulty holding a job. A poor decision made as a teenager has led to a tragic life filled with much unnecessary misery.

I know of another individual who became hooked on Internet pornography. He had a wife and four children. His addiction eventually resulted in him planning a rendezvous with a fourteen-year-old-girl that he met on an Internet chat site. The meeting turned out to be with an undercover police agent. His addiction and decision ultimately led to the loss of his family, the loss of his Church membership, the loss of his job as a schoolteacher, and the loss of his good name and standing in the community. Talk about self-inflicted trials and misery brought about by making poor decisions.

Now, as previously noted, there are other trials and difficulties that we will all experience in life that are not because of poor decisions we make. Sometimes stuff happens that we have little or no control over.

During one period of his life, a major trial came to the Prophet Joseph in the form of his imprisonment in Liberty Jail. While suffering extreme deprivation for many months in that dimly-lit dungeon, Joseph was still in relatively good physical health and was blessed by the knowledge that he had a wonderful family and a good marriage with Emma. He had close friends. He was well aware that thousands of Saints loved and revered him and were praying for him. But in spite of the fact that he had these and many other little bluebirds sitting on his shoulders (which under normal circumstances would have lifted his spirit upwards toward happiness), the reality was that he still had a huge rock sitting on him, a major trial holding him down, making it next to impossible for him to hear the cheerful, uplifting song of those little birds.

Freedom and agency provide us with fertile ground for growing happiness. A loss of freedom is a major happiness killer. Such a loss is especially difficult to endure when totally undeserved, as was the case with the Prophet Joseph Smith.

No question about it, this was an extremely difficult and sad time in Joseph's life, and there was nothing much he could do to change it. Apparently it was a period, designated by the Lord, for him to learn greater patience, humility, and reliance upon God. Although Joseph would ultimately be provided with feelings of peace and comfort from the Spirit during this trial, as he would be in all his trials, he still did not enjoy many feelings of great happiness and joy during this most difficult time in his life.

During one period of my own life, I experienced a trial related to my employment. I had been working for a large international oil company for many years. The company had been cutting back on employees and positions, thus reducing the chances of promotion while at the same time requiring more responsibility and more output from the remaining employees.

I was beginning to feel stressed and quite bored with my job, having repeated the same accounting and administrative reports every month for a number of years. I knew that possibilities for a job change within the company had been eliminated and I still had two years to go before I could take early retirement at age fifty. If I left the company for another job before that point I would lose a modest pension as well as some much needed health insurance benefits.

While I greatly desired to leave the company and find a different job at which I could be much happier, reason told me that I just couldn't afford to lose those retirement benefits. I had to hang on for another two years.

Although things were far from great at work, during this same period wonderful things were happening in other areas of my life. My family life was great and my health was good. For the second time in my life I had been blessed with the calling of bishop, which gave me the opportunity to feel a lot of love and to experience an exceptionally large dose of joy that comes from serving others.

In spite of the fact that I was feeling frustrated and basically unhappy at work, I had so many other good things happening in my life that I can honestly say that this was a very happy time in my life. Although my situation in life wasn't as perfect as I would have liked, I still felt very, very blessed.

Certainly this trial in my life was not nearly as difficult as the one that the Prophet was required to endure in Liberty Jail. Nevertheless, imagine what my life might have been like during this period if, besides being basically unhappy at work, I had also been suffering from an unhappy marriage, poor health, and severe financial worries. Rather than being basically happy, my unhappiness might have been close to a Liberty Jail experience. Fortunately, however, I had made certain that those areas of my life over which I could assert some control were producing happiness, not unhappiness. Maybe things weren't so great at work, but with a dozen or more little bluebirds singing on my shoulders, how could I complain?

In a similar manner, you can also expect to experience some sad times in your life, caused by extremely difficult trials that perhaps you can do little about. This is your refining time. Don't lose hope during this period, it will eventually pass. *Just make certain you learn the lessons you are supposed to during these difficult times so your suffering isn't in vain.* Also, remember that there will be other times in your life, not so far ahead, that you can experience much happiness and joy in spite of the trials that come your way *if* you have fully applied in your life those principles that create happiness.

In Conclusion: The Secret to a Happier Life

The eighteen happiness principles that we have looked at in this book are certainly not an all-inclusive listing. There are many other sources of happiness that we could have discussed in some detail. For example, studies show that people with close friends are happier than those without any. This is particularly true during one's school years. After marriage, busy family schedules often curtail the time we have to nurture outside friendships as much as we would like, and our spouse and children typically become our best friends (as they should be). This is yet another reason for working hard to make your marriage and family life a great one.

Another common characteristic of all who describe themselves as being very happy, or extremely happy, is that they regularly take time to count their blessings. They have a gratitude attitude. Earlier in my life, I made a list of some of my many blessings. I would carry this list with me in my wallet. When problems would crop up and I started to feel down, I would simply pull out my list, read it over and remind myself of just how blessed I really was. Although I am not overly wealthy in material things, with so many far more valuable blessings having been showered upon me, I often feel like I am the richest man on earth. It's pretty difficult to keep feeling sorry for myself when I remind myself of this fact. I no longer carry that written list of blessings in my wallet; that list has been transferred over and is now written in my heart and soul.

As gratitude swells up in our hearts, there will be times when our prayers to God will be entirely prayers of thanksgiving. The more time you spend counting your blessings and expressing thanks to God for those blessings, the greater will be the feelings of happiness and joy that come into your life.

There are many ways we can increase feelings of happiness in our lives, but the best way, the greatest secret to a happy life, is clearly expressed and summarized by President Spencer W. Kimball:

> "What is the price of happiness?" One might be surprised at the simplicity of the answer. The treasure house of happiness is unlocked to those who live the gospel of Jesus Christ in its purity and simplicity. Like a mariner without stars, like a traveler without a compass, is the person who moves along through life without a plan. The assurance of supreme happiness, the certainty of a successful life here and of exaltation and eternal life hereafter, come to those who plan to live their lives in complete harmony with the gospel of Jesus Christ—and then consistently follow the course they have set.[1]

Yes, the secret to living a truly happy life is found in simply living the gospel of Jesus Christ, the perfect plan of happiness.

As our time together now comes to a close, I pray that feelings of inner peace, celestial love, and humble gratitude may forever fill your heart. May you be successful in your quest to capture many of those wonderful little bluebirds of happiness. And as you increase the feelings of happiness in your own life, I hope you will take the time to share the secrets of your happy life with others. God's plan is for everyone. May you be an instrument in His hands in helping as many of His children as possible to come to a clear understanding of His magnificent plan of happiness for mankind. God bless and be with you always!

Notes

1. Spencer W. Kimball, *The Miracle of Forgiveness* (Salt Lake City, Utah: Bookcraft, 1969), 259.

About the Author

Gregory R. Wille was born and raised in the Chicago, Illinois, area. Growing up, he played Little League baseball and high school basketball, and earned his Eagle Scout award. As a young man he served a full-time LDS mission to Australia and afterward graduated from BYU with a degree in accounting. He met his eternal companion, Shelley, in a BYU ward, and they were married in the Salt Lake Temple. They are the parents of two daughters and four sons and are currently grandparents to seven very active little grandchildren. Their six children have served missions to England, Norway, Ukraine, France, Australia, and Mexico.

Brother Wille has worked for a CPA firm, a large international oil company, and several other smaller firms, as an accountant, administrative coordinator, and chief financial officer. In the Church, he has served as a stake mission president, twice as a bishop, and in many other teaching and leadership positions. Next to his love for God and the Savior, his greatest joy comes in knowing that families are forever.

Sidebar quotes are from the following sources:

www.madwed.com

www.wisdomquotes.com

www.betterworld.net

www.heartquotes.net

www.quotegarden.com

www.quoteworld.org

www.quotationspage.com

www.more-selfesteem.com

www.entplaza.com

http://ifwallscouldtalkdecorating.com

Elizabeth Knowles, *The Oxford Dictionary of Quotations*, (New York: Oxford University Press, 1999).

Meiji Stewart, *Happiness is an Inside Job* (Del Mar, California: Keep Coming Back Company, 1997).